EXILE

EXILE

Rejecting America and Finding the World

Belén Fernández

OR Books
New York · London

All rights information: rights@orbooks.com
Visit our website at www.orbooks.com

First printing 2019

Library of Congress Cataloging-in-Publication Data: A catalog record for this book is
available from the Library of Congress.
British Library Cataloging in Publication Data: A catalog record for this book is available
from the British Library.

Typeset by Lapiz Digital Services, Chennai, India.

Map by Pocomeloso. All photos courtesy the author © Belén Fernández

paperback ISBN 978-1-68219-185-9 • ebook ISBN 978-1-68219-189-7

For my parents, as always

CONTENTS

The Travels of Belén

Albania	Georgia
Argentina	Greece
Bosnia	Honduras
Colombia	Iran
Cuba	Italy
Ecuador	Kyrgyzstan
Ethiopia	Lebanon

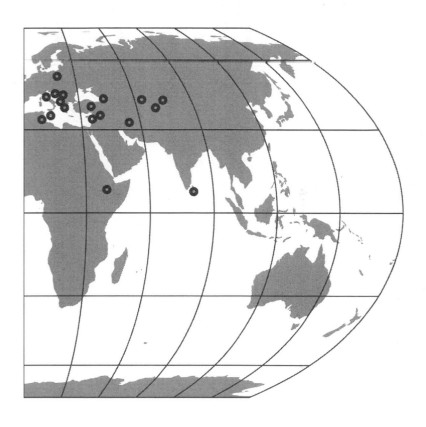

Malta	Syria
Mexico	Tajikistan
Morocco	Tunisia
Poland	Turkey
Serbia	Uzbekistan
Spain	Venezuela
Sri Lanka	United States

PREFACE

Once upon a time, James Baldwin wrote that "perhaps home is not a place but simply an irrevocable condition."

This, to me, is an appealing conceptualization, as it spares me from having to think too much about where—after more than 15 years of being constantly on the move—home might be. It also definitively absolves me of the need to resurrect any warm and fuzzy feelings vis-à-vis the place of my birth and upbringing, i.e. the United States, the global superpower that has specialized in making much of the planet an unfit abode for its inhabitants via a combination of perennial war, environmental despoliation, and punitive economic policies resulting in mass migration.

To be sure, "nowhere" has never been an enormously well-received response, among international immigration and passport control officers, to the question of where I live. I suppose I could say "everywhere," but that would be distinctly obnoxious, especially in light of the fact that the majority of the world's population is decidedly more constrained by borders than a U.S. passport holder.

Nor does my lifestyle elicit approval from folks concerned that, without a fixed residence, one cannot actually *be*. And yet some of these same people have no qualms telling migrants and refugees to go "home"—even when a physical place called "home" may be one that precludes existence itself, and consequently the irrevocable condition.

As it so happens, I came across a similar Baldwin-esque sentiment in the Bosnian capital of Sarajevo during the winter of 2018, where I parked myself for two grey months and attempted daily jogs on a path by the Miljacka river, clad in a hideous pileup of sweaters, scarves, and socks. These outings, characterized by collisions with patches of ice and elderly pedestrians, were generally accompanied by intense feelings of self-pity and loneliness. They were also punctuated by reminders, in the form of mortar shell scars dating from the siege of Sarajevo in the mid-1990s, that I should shut the fuck up about my own perceived plight.

On one jog, I discovered a graffito on the asphalt stating something to the effect of: "Home is where you are." Though it may very well have been directed at the object of the graffiti artist's affection, I preferred to interpret it as a personalized form of reassurance—at least, that is, until everything in Sarajevo was buried under mounds of snow and I opted instead to adopt the mantra: "Home is where the stockpile of wine is."

Fortuitously, the apartment I was renting in the city—not far from the bridge where the 1914 assassination of Austrian Archduke Franz Ferdinand sparked World War I—was located just above the home of a Bosnian family comprised of two veterans of the siege of the '90s, who saw to it that I was never anything less than jammed full of spinach-and-cheese pies. Their young daughter Uma taught me essential Bosnian words like "wine," "spinach-and-cheese pie," and "catastrophe," and also introduced me to the joys of a Michael Jackson video dance game.

While my own current irrevocable condition appears to be itinerant—and my exile from the U.S. definitive—the generosity with which the world has received me would seem to indicate that home is where the humans are.

— *Belén Fernández*
Sarajevo, December 2018

1. BEGINNINGS

In 1993, at the age of eleven, I entered the seventh grade at St. Louis Catholic School in Austin, Texas. This was my third Catholic school in a row despite the fact that neither of my parents were discernibly religious. The first had been Our Lady of Lourdes in Bethesda, Maryland, where I learned to spell "Our Lady of Lourdes" and progressed to writing short stories about a flatulent bat named Blaster. The second was St. Theresa's in Austin, where we had moved when my father decided that he would prefer to carry out his professional duties as a reporter far away from his publication's headquarters in Washington, D.C., such that no one could verify he was working when he said he was or interfere with his spontaneous reinvention as a cowboy.

The third and last of my Catholic institutions, St. Louis was nestled among the picturesque strip malls of north Austin and run by a totalitarian regime according to whose divine knowledge my dog was not going to heaven, tinted lip balm was a venial sin, and misperformance of the Pledge of Allegiance was tantamount to blasphemy. The tedium of earthly existence was eased on the occasional Free Dress Day, although I quickly discovered via public humiliation and a trip to the principal's office that "freedom" did not always extend past the school uniform colors of green and white.

Spiritual indoctrination techniques aside, St. Louis served as a fine example of what is known as education in the United States—where a focus on exam-driven memorization often precludes a more integrated world-view. My history teacher Mrs. Conway, for example, went so far as to distribute a practice copy of each test beforehand—which meant that I spent junior high simply memorizing and regurgitating sequences of multiple-choice answers (B, A, C, D, B, E, and so on) rather than, say, wondering why the all-hallowed founding fathers of the U.S. were slave owners.

As in any country, the history of the U.S. is written by the ruling class in accordance with its own interests. The difference is that the U.S., despite being founded on slavery and the genocide of Native Americans, presents itself as the global model for greatness—a position that is unilaterally interpreted as a carte blanche to bomb, invade, and otherwise enlighten the rest of the world as it sees fit. In U.S. mythology, the experiences of its founding victims are cast as free-standing tragedies that allude in no way whatsoever to the putrid core of the U.S. enterprise, while the more contemporary slaughter-fests in Hiroshima, Nagasaki, Vietnam, Iraq, and beyond are just Things That Had to Be Done.

Long before I grasped any of this, my childhood was pleasant, characterized by pre-technological activities like digging up worms in the garden and dropping the dog from the second-floor landing (she nonetheless survived 14 years). I did suffer from early-onset list-making neurosis, most likely a genetic inheritance from my father and grandfather, who used overzealous checklists to exert symbolic control over the universe. A stack of papers in wobbly handwriting enumerated my daily duties, ready to be marked off: wake up, brush teeth, go to school, come back from school, eat ice-cream, etc. When I learned of the existence of the Amazon River, my lists expanded to include preparations for my eventual journey there, with notes to investigate how many orders of Kentucky Fried Chicken I would need to pack.

Occasionally, I took up all-American causes. When I was six, I fashioned a lucky charm out of clay and prayed over it in the basement for the duration of the 1988 Super Bowl, causing the Washington Redskins to vanquish the Denver Broncos. My magic rituals on behalf of the Dukakis-Benson campaign that same year were less successful, resulting in the presidency of George H. W. Bush.

My brother, three years younger than me, was another subject for experiments. After training him to climb out of his crib, to my parents' great dismay, I dreamed up projects like breaking his finger in order to experience the exhilaration of calling the ambulance. His finger didn't break; I called the ambulance anyway. Indeed, if there is any doubt that I am to blame for the subsequent disintegration of the fraternal relationship, there is confirmation in old Betamax footage of me trailing my brother dictatorially around the backyard, demanding shrilly: "WHAT DOES THE PIGGY SAY, JOEY? WHAT DOES THE PIGGY SAY?!"

St. Louis Catholic School marked the end of childhood fun and games, particularly when classmates informed me that, not only did I have hair on my legs, I also had a mustache and insufficient breasts. My time there was however not entirely wasted. Shortly before my twelfth birthday I acquired a boyfriend named Rómulo, with whom I spent many hours seated on the floor of the local library after school, holding hands in tortured silence. When my ride would arrive, we would exchange the obligatory kiss on the mouth and declaration of love, and then I would dart outside.

During one such passionate encounter, we were interrupted by a classmate with the last name Meléndez, who inquired as to the origins of my own Fernández. For whatever reason, I consulted a map on the library wall and decided that the Mexican state of Coahuila was as good an answer to this question as any.

Granted, this is a dull memory to conserve for various decades. But it only surfaced long after I had left the U.S. in 2003, when I was trying to recall if I'd ever possessed any sort of identity beyond being that person who wasted her life writing a book about Thomas Friedman (conclusion: not really). In any case, the Fernández family had nothing to do with Coahuila—something I did in fact know at the age of eleven, especially because I had once commandeered a family tree that dated back to the thirteenth century and had appointed a relative named Luis Centurión as our official house ghost.

Our modern family history started with Joseph Fernández, my father and the son of the late Joseph and Jeanette Fernández, who had both been born in the Ybor City neighborhood of Tampa, Florida, both to fathers named José Fernández. These two families hailed from assorted regions of Spain and Cuba.

Some of the ancestors were more colorful than others, as I was able to confirm when my dad at last managed, in 2017, to take time out of his retirement schedule of repeatedly reading *Don Quixote* to complete the memoir he had begun 17 years before. This memoir had served as his excuse for a roaming sabbatical from his job as a correspondent for The Bureau of National Affairs, Inc. (subsequently acquired by Bloomberg). His paternal Abuelo José, for one, "was convinced that using the toilet was not good for the plumbing," and thus saw to it that his wife always urinated in a Café Bustelo can. This same José, it turned out, had belittled my father's college degree: "Better to have knocked around like Don Quixote and Sancho, learning from life," he said. Hence, perhaps, the subsequent choice of reading materials.

Meanwhile, my dad's other Abuelo José, known as "El Boy," had stabbed a fellow cigar factory worker in Ybor City for insulting the family and had then been shipped off by his sisters to Cuba in the early 1900s, where he found refuge with the Centurión relatives in the eastern Cuban town of Jiguaní until the charges against him cleared—at which point he returned to Tampa and took up work with the Mafia boss Santo Trafficante. Nearly a century later, in 2006, I traveled with a few friends to Jiguaní to visit the contemporary crop of relatives, who hosted us in their homes and treated us to heaps of fried pork rinds along with family tales, such as The Tragedy of Not Being Able to Remodel the Bathroom Since 1962 Because Fidel Castro.

My own grandparents, for their part, did their best to de-Hispanicize their offspring, and my grandfather facilitated patriotic assimilation by joining the armed forces, thanks to which he was able to participate in not only the D-Day landings at Normandy but also the Korean and Vietnam wars. Other career highlights included briefing U.S. defense secretary Robert McNamara during the Cuban Missile Crisis and serving as the director of military intelligence for the U.S. Southern Command in the Panama Canal Zone in the 1970s, in which capacity he enjoyed frequent meetings with Manuel Noriega, the soon-to-be dictator of Panama. A decades-long CIA asset despite his well-known involvement in the international drug trade, Noriega ran afoul of Bush senior in the late 1980s, and consequently the U.S. military rained death and destruction upon impoverished sections of Panama City under the euphemism Operation Just Cause.[1] United States officials highlighted the justness of their cause by pointing to a stash of

---

1   As with other bellicose U.S. escapades, the media by and large leapt aboard the "Just Cause" bandwagon, dutifully demonizing Noriega and lowballing Panamanian casualty estimates, which some observers put in the thousands. The media watch group Fairness and Accuracy in Reporting (FAIR) noted at the time that the poor Panama City neighborhood of El Chorillo had been pulverized to the point of being referred to by ambulance drivers as "Little Hiroshima" (Cohen, Jeff. "How Television Sold the Panama Invasion." *FAIR*, 1 January 1990. https://fair.org/extra/how-television-sold-the-panama-invasion/) Overall, the lightning-quick success of Just Cause helped the American public overcome that pesky affliction known as Vietnam Syndrome, and served as a test run for the Persian Gulf War. It also served as a warning to Nicaragua of what might be in store for that country if the Sandinistas remained in power.

cocaine discovered in a house that Noriega frequented. The cocaine turned out to be tamales wrapped in banana leaves, although a Pentagon spokeswoman noted that these, too, were problematic: "It's a substance they use in voodoo rituals."[2]

His role as imperial servant notwithstanding, my granddad had a soft spot for Castro, Che Guevara, and other regional figures whose irritating legacy of sticking it to the empire could not be suppressed by any number of U.S.-backed juntas, dictators, and death squads. The fruits of his military service were on clear display at the end of his life, which he spent dashing nude through the corridors of a Texas nursing home, detecting potential invasions by the Mexican Air Force and reporting his fellow nursing home residents for suspected communist activity involving their oxygen tanks.

My mother's father, also a Floridian and a former Air Force pilot, was more secure in his ideological foundations. When I was dragged to the Florida panhandle for a disconcerting visit in 2009, this granddad informed me that, not only was Barack Obama himself a communist, the U.S. should have obliterated both Vietnam and Iraq from the face of the earth. This particular prescription for world justice was delivered without a hint of rancor, much in the manner that one might suggest watering the plants in the backyard.

My mother's mother, with whom we had severed contact early, presided over more DIY forms of belligerence such as breaking the hip of an elderly aunt in a staircase showdown and threatening her own daughter with a gun. After being temporarily confiscated by authorities, the firearm was

---

2   "OOPS! : Noriega 'Cocaine' Was Tamales." The *Los Angeles Times*, 23 January 1990. http://articles .latimes.com/1990-01-23/news/mn-757_1_manuel-a-noriega

returned to my grandmother in accordance with the inalienable rights of U.S. citizens to militarized sociopathy. Other relatives on my mother's side meanwhile weren't sure what to make of my father's last name and were concerned he might be black. Somehow, my mom emerged from this milieu with logic intact as well as an impressive range of positive human emotions.

Following a mercifully brief post-9/11 upsurge in patriotic sentiment, my parents decided they could live without the War on Terror, and the ensuing reign of Obama—the king of drone strikes, deportations, and other damage—definitively cured them of any notion that the Democratic Party was slightly better than the alternative.[3] Some years after I abandoned the U.S., my parents relocated to Argentina, then to Panama, and finally to Barcelona, where they pledged not to budge and where my dad augmented his *Don Quixote* regimen by inaugurating a hobby of postcard-writing to Beelzebub and Mephistopheles, c/o the White House and the office of the prime minister of Israel.

My brother went the other way and inserted himself into U.S. Special Operations forces, a not entirely astonishing career choice given his inundation as a child by every conceivable piece of military paraphernalia from the grandfathers, including a camouflage beekeeping outfit. Perhaps he had also adopted the distinctly American philosophy that life is a video

---

3   Obama authorized ten times more drone strikes than his warmongering predecessor George W. Bush (Purkiss, Jessica and Jack Serle. "Obama's covert drone war in numbers: Ten times more strikes than Bush." *The Bureau of Investigative Journalism*, 17 January 2017. https://www.thebureauinvestigates.com/stories/2017-01-17/obamas-covert-drone-war-in-numbers-ten-times-more-strikes-than-bush). As ABC News noted in 2016, citing governmental data, the Obama administration also "deported more [people] than the sum of all the presidents of the 20th century" (Marshall, Serena. "Obama Has Deported More People Than Any Other President." *ABC News*, 29 August 2016. https://abcnews.go.com/Politics/obamas-deportation-policy-numbers/story?id=41715661).

game. As he himself insinuated, Special Force–hood and the preposterous muscles that came along with it constituted a symbolic triumph against the bullies of his school years. In practice, this meant that the rare familial rendezvous henceforth consisted of me hiding in a closet while my brother exhibited his biceps and railed against the douchebags of the international community who had objected to the U.S. use of flesh-incinerating white phosphorus in Syria and Iraq.[4]

* * *

Back in 1967, Martin Luther King, Jr. denounced the U.S. government as "the greatest purveyor of violence in the world," with the Vietnam War "the symptom of a far deeper malady within the American spirit." Indeed, he lamented, the U.S. was "on the side of the wealthy, and the secure, while we create a hell for the poor."[5]

Half a century later, the scholar Roxanne Dunbar-Ortiz touched on a couple of other enduring characteristics of that same American spirit in her book *An Indigenous Peoples' History of the United States*:

> ...the endless [U.S.] wars of aggression and occupations; the trillions spent on war machinery, military bases, and personnel instead of social services and quality public education; the gross profits of corporations, each of which has greater resources and funds than more than half the countries in the world yet pay minimal taxes and provide few jobs for U.S. citizens; the repression of generation after generation of activists who seek to change the system; the incarceration of the

---

4   "Iraq/Syria: Danger From U.S. White Phosphorus." Human Rights Watch, 14 June 2017. https://www.hrw.org/news/2017/06/14/iraq-syria-danger-us-white-phosphorus

5   Quoted in Hedin, Benjamin. "Martin Luther King, Jr.'s searing antiwar speech, fifty years later." *The New Yorker*, 3 April 2017. https://www.newyorker.com/culture/culture-desk/martin-luther-king-jr-s-searing-antiwar-speech-fifty-years-later

poor, particularly descendants of enslaved Africans; the individualism, carefully inculcated, that on the one hand produces self-blame for personal failure and on the other exalts ruthless dog-eat-dog competition for possible success, even though it rarely results; and high rates of suicide, drug abuse, alcoholism, sexual violence against women and children, homelessness, dropping out of school, and gun violence.[6]

However much I myself would come to dislike the U.S., then, I had precious little to gripe about compared to fellow Americans who were sentenced to life in prison for shoplifting three belts from a department store, or killed by law enforcement personnel for engaging in any number of Activities While Black—from running to walking to driving to breathing.[7] Being Chained Up in Jail While Black had also been known to elicit potentially homicidal impulses in representatives of the state; as the *Washington Post* editorial board diplomatically put it following one such case in Virginia in 2015, "the coroner found that the fact that Natasha McKenna was shot repeatedly with a stun gun while she was shackled was part of the mix leading to her death."[8]

---

6   Dunbar-Ortiz, Roxanne. *An Indigenous Peoples' History of the United States.* Boston: Beacon Press, 2014. Pp. 229–30.

7   For belt theft, see Turner, Jennifer. "What a Waste." American Civil Liberties Union, 13 November 2013. https://www.aclu.org/blog/smart-justice/mass-incarceration/what-waste?redirect=blog/mass-incarceration/what-waste
    For lethal responses to Activities While Black, see: Andone, Dakin and Carolyn Sung. "Bodycam footage shows Utah police shoot man as he runs away." *CNN*, 9 October 2017. https://edition.cnn.com/2017/10/08/us/patrick-harmon-utah-police-shooting/index.html; "Houston officer kills unarmed man walking with trousers down." *BBC News*, 28 March 2018. https://www.bbc.com/news/world-us-canada-43574249; "Police officer who shot dead Philando Castile acquitted of all charges." Associated Press, 16 June 2017. https://www.theguardian.com/us-news/2017/jun/16/philando-castile-death-police-officer-not-guilty; Taibbi, Matt. *I Can't Breathe: A Killing on Bay Street.* New York: Penguin Random House, 2018.

8   *Washington Post* Editorial Board. "In Fairfax case, death by 'excited delirium.'" The *Washington Post*, 27 April 2015. https://www.washingtonpost.com/opinions/death-by-excited-delirium/2015/04/27/4f5f7a86-ed27-11e4-8abc-d6aa3bad79dd_story.html?utm_term=.5e8c1947f14f

Lest folks start to view the state itself as public enemy number one, however, more convenient menaces are regularly trotted out. In addition to the usual domestic suspects—blacks, poor people, immigrants, and so on—the wider world has proved fertile terrain for the manufacture of any number of freedom-imperiling demons. I personally came along too late to fully appreciate the whole Soviet scare, but I was introduced at the age of eight to the concept of Saddam Hussein, who, my fourth-grade teacher at St. Theresa's informed us, could bomb our classroom at any minute.

This was during Operation Desert Storm, less than a decade after the U.S. had helped enable the very same Saddam Hussein in various chemical weapons endeavors. The U.S. has a habit of selectively choosing the time and circumstances for an ally to become an enemy and vice versa, perhaps more so than any other modern nation. As Oxford University's Peter Frankopan noted in *The Silk Roads: A New History of the World*, the U.S. "responded with silence" in the mid-1980s when United Nations reports indicated that Iraq was using chemical weapons against its own civilians. It was furthermore "highly embarrassing that Iraq's production capability, as one senior American officer pointed out, was 'primarily [derived] from Western firms, including possibly a U.S. foreign subsidiary'"—which clearly "raised uncomfortable questions about complicity in Saddam's acquisition and use" of internationally banned items.[9]

Once the winds had shifted, Iraq became a target not only of U.S. bombs but also U.S. sanctions—which could be weapons of mass destruction themselves. When confronted with reports in 1996 that half a million Iraqi children had perished on account of the sanctions regime, then-U.S.

---

9   Frankopan, Peter. *The Silk Roads: A New History of the World*. New York: Vintage Books, 2017, p. 460.

Ambassador to the UN Madeleine Albright reasoned: "We think the price is worth it."[10]

As soon as I learned of the threat that Iraq posed to my fourth-grade class-room, I composed a letter to Saddam in which I told him about my horses and asked him to please keep his missiles to himself. Though I never heard back from the man directly, I did hear from a certain American soldier by the last name of McGee, a participant in Desert Storm whom St. Theresa's had assigned me as a pen pal—as it was apparently never too early to start supporting our troops. PFC McGee kindly sent me some desert sand and Saudi coins, and I corrected his punctuation and grammar with multi-colored highlighters.

When in 2003 it was once again deemed existentially imperative to go after Saddam, I was in my senior year at Columbia University in New York and had settled into a daily routine of debilitating panic attacks, having returned from junior year abroad at the University of Rome to find that my homeland resembled a large-scale lab experiment on how to best crush the human soul. (Granted, Iraqis who were about to be literally crushed, and Afghans who were already mid-crushing, had far more substantial complaints to register.) It was not that the U.S. had been fundamentally altered in my absence during the post-9/11 tsunami of patriotic cliché, but rather that the rigidity and joylessness of the place were more glaringly obvious after a year in a Roman neighborhood where everything closed for four hours in the middle of the day to allow for leisurely gorging and nap-time. The self-assured grace with which Italians seemed to move through the universe—even while constantly spewing penis- and testicle-related

---

10 For video clip see "Democracy Now! Confronts Madeleine Albright on the Iraq Sanctions: Was It Worth the Price?" *Democracy Now!*, 30 July 2004. https://www.democracynow.org/2004/7/30/democracy_now_confronts_madeline_albright_on

expletives—made it increasingly difficult to view the U.S. public as anything but a bumbling mass sorely mismatched with earthly ecosystems.

This wasn't my first rodeo when it came to panic attacks. Since elementary school, I had periodically misdiagnosed myself with epilepsy, heart attacks, and other conditions that led to lengthy hyperventilation sessions in bathroom stalls. It's possible that I was simply doing my best to keep in line with the American mantra that There Is Always Something Wrong With You, but the common denominator in the anxiety attacks seemed to be the fear that no one would help me—hardly an irrational sentiment in a system predicated on individual isolation and a general estrangement from humanity. And while Italy may not always be the most helpful society on the planet—witness the boatloads of refugees left to drown in recent years by the Italian coast guard—the ubiquity of cheap wine made it a suitable spot to sit out the inaugural year of the War on Terror, launched just before I departed for Rome in 2001.[11]

Repatriation the following year reintroduced me to manic air-conditioning and other joys of an alienated society, where capitalism was tied up with the criminalization and pathologization of normal human behavior that left the criminally diseased system itself untouched. Forget empathy, communal bonds, attention spans unobliterated by technology, or the cultivation of citizens that might effectively oppose state violence at home or abroad. The U.S. has long had other priorities, such as the commodification of everything under the sun and the maintenance of a sheeplike media to glorify imperial bellicosity, as was the case with giddy news coverage of the pummeling of Iraq.

---

11 See, for example, Osborne, Samuel. "Horrific phone calls reveal how Italian Coast Guard let dozens of refugees drown." The *Independent*, 8 May 2017. https://www.independent.co.uk/news/world/europe/italian-navy-lets-refugees-drown-migrants-crisis-asylum-seekers-mediterranean-sea-a7724156.html

The shortage of compassion across the board has worked out well for the arms and pharmaceutical industries, among other businesses for whom unhinged environments are an ideal market, and the national landscape has proved ever more optimal for school shootings—one of those phenomena that is somehow magically absent from many of the Inferior Countries of the globe. Nor do people in most countries require Gwyneth Paltrow to sell them salt for $78.[12]

And while the ascent of Donald Trump has been bewailed as a gigantic accident by those who insist that the U.S. is pure and well-meaning at heart, a mere glance at the national track record of bipartisan support for eternal war, bigotry, American exceptionalism, and the deification of money suggests that America had all the right preexisting conditions and then some.

* * *

In September 2003, I escaped the U.S. again after a short post-graduation stint as an office peon in Austin had caused me to conclude that I had no choice but to pursue certification as a teacher of English as a foreign language, which was clearly best done on the Greek island of Crete. A month-long program in the Cretan city of Chania produced the desired teaching certificate, which I never used, and a traveling companion in the form of Amelia, a classmate in the course. Born in Rzeszów, Poland, she had moved to New Jersey as a child, when her parents opted to abandon the domain of the Warsaw Pact and check out what life was like in places where the basic necessities of survival were not free.

---

12 Refer to the website of Paltrow's goop "lifestyle brand" for an array of money-squandering (and potentially life-harming https://www.cnbc.com/2018/10/29/gwyneth-paltrows-goop-reported-to-uk-watchdogs-overadvertising.html) shopping ideas: https://goop.com/. As of winter 2018, "Bath Salts for Inner Peace" were available for $78 (https://goop.com/beauty/bath-body/the-beauty-benefits-of-salt-they-may-surprise-you/).

In Chania, Amelia and I discovered the perks of hitchhiking, which would be a primary pastime for both of us in the coming years and would spare us the need to devote too much time to earning money. We first headed to Poland, where we endured continuous coercive feeding by her grandmother, a veteran of a Siberian labor camp in World War II. Amelia's grandfather had also done time in a labor camp, a German one, and possessed a repertoire of German anthems to show for it, some of which were belted out suddenly in the middle of the night. From our weeks in Poland I learned that it was possible to cure any number of illnesses with the right amount of hard liquor and garlic; it was, however, still cold outside, and—once our visions of restaurant dishwashing jobs had failed to pan out and we had narrowly circumvented conscription into the Herbalife cult—we determined that southern Spain was, meteorologically speaking, a far more reasonable place to be.

We selected the coastal Andalucían town of Nerja as our preliminary destination based on the presence there of a branch of my father's family that had not emigrated to Cuba and that he had tracked down in the course of his memoir investigations. This family presided over a café in the town center and included three sisters of varying degrees of ancientness, the eldest having been imprisoned for six years in the 1940s for providing assistance to anti-Franco guerrillas operating out of nearby mountains. Two brothers had been summarily shot for guerrilla activity. Through an employee of the Nerja café, Amelia and I met a Moroccan construction worker called Abdul, who inexplicably invited us to reside rent-free in his home in the neighboring village of Frigiliana and procured jobs for us at the local avocado packing facility, where the Spanish avocado bosses commanded us to work *como una máquina* and offered supplementary encouragement in the form of boxed wine and cognac in plastic cups.

The living arrangement in Frigiliana succeeded until Abdul's brother moved in and commenced a routine of smashing beer bottles on the floor, which rendered walking difficult, and inserting needles into a photograph of Abdul, Amelia, and me that hung on the wall. Amelia and I relocated to Turkey, though we did return to the western Mediterranean the following year for a trans-Morocco hitchhiking jaunt that involved a visit to Abdul's extended family in a hamlet in the country's interior, where we were occasionally permitted to stop ingesting things long enough to participate in impromptu dance parties.

Numerous ensuing international hitchhiking expeditions enabled us to confirm that, while the planet may have been going to hell, there were still some damn fine people on it. Relatively rare was the occasion on which we had to leap out of a moving vehicle to thwart molestation; ditto for finding ourselves in the middle of nowhere in the middle of the night in the cab of an 18-wheeler with a driver who wanted to sleep in our laps. Meanwhile, the potential for novel experiences was always high, as when I was trampled by a bull after a driver armed with a vat of tequila had convinced me to participate in a Mexican village bullfight.

One of our earliest achievements was a five-day hitchhiking journey from Spain to Istanbul, for which we relied entirely on the outline of Europe on the five-euro bill and made a single stop mid-Serbia, at what we assumed was a thermal bath complex but turned out to be a treatment center for rheumatic persons. After some heated negotiations with the man behind the reception desk, we were permitted to take part—in our bras and underwear—in a water aerobics class led by a giant Serb named Little Joe, who paced up and down the side of the pool smoking cigarettes and barking orders.

Other trips were more sobering. In 2006, Amelia and I hitchhiked from Turkey through Syria to Lebanon, arriving a month after the end of the 34-day Israeli assault that killed some 1,200 people—the majority of whom were civilians. The U.S. had rush-shipped bombs to the Israel Defense Forces (IDF) during the onslaught, while U.S. officials advocated against a too-swift ceasefire and President Bush invented words like "Hezbollian."[13] The result: a landscape of craters and rubble across much of the country where apartment blocks and other infrastructure had once stood.

My regrettable nationality notwithstanding, we were picked up and carted home for meals and other kindnesses by an array of individuals, including ones who had lost family members and friends to U.S.-backed carnage. Offers of free accommodations were sometimes complicated by the presence of unexploded cluster bombs on the premises in question. As Human Rights Watch reported regarding Israel's use of such munitions in 2006: "The IDF rained an estimated four million submunitions on south Lebanon, the vast majority over the final three days when Israel knew a settlement was imminent."[14]

In 2009, Amelia and I traversed Ecuador, Colombia, and Venezuela, taking advantage of the final locale to have all of our health care needs (real and imagined) attended to gratis by Venezuelan and Cuban medics in the Barrio Adentro clinics established by then-president Hugo Chavez. A female Cuban doctor from none other than Guantánamo province—who had worked in Afghanistan and various African countries—not only honored our requests for superfluous ultrasounds but also provided us with a

---

13 For more about these rush shipments, see Cloud, David S. and Helene Cooper. "U.S. Speeds Up Bomb Delivery for the Israelis." *New York Times*, 22 July 2006. https://www.nytimes .com/2006/07/22/world/middleeast/22military.html; for Bush's expansion of English lexicon see "President Bush Meets with Bipartisan Members of Congress on the G8 Summit." U.S. State Department website archive, 18 July 2006. https://georgewbush-whitehouse.archives.gov/news/ releases/2006/07/20060718-4.html

14 "Flooding South Lebanon: Israel's Use of Cluster Munitions in Lebanon in July and August 2006." Human Rights Watch, 16 February 2008. https://www.hrw.org/report/2008/02/16/flood-ing-south-lebanon/israels-use-cluster-munitions-lebanon-july-and-august-2006

sheet of mind-altering allergy pills. She assured us that Cuba would never deny medical services to citizens or Green Card holders of the embargoing, occupying power. She went on to observe that, like the Americans, Cuban doctors also operated in conflict zones—but to save lives.

Other highlights of our Venezuelan sojourn included a February referendum that pitted *Sí* against *No*. Amelia and I inserted ourselves into the *Sí* campaign in the Venezuelan state of Anzoátegui east of Caracas, for which our duties consisted of dancing in the back of a pickup truck to songs about Chávez, *el pueblo*, and the imminent victory of the *Sí*.

Amelia eventually settled on the Yucatán peninsula, while I continued to eschew a fixed residence with the help of periodic influxes of Qatari money for op-eds. There hasn't been a great deal of logic to my international wanderings, though a certain kind of hangover has proved productive in terms of manic acquisition of bargain plane tickets to places like Kyrgyzstan. The need to be in continuous motion is, it seems, some sort of severe form of commitment-phobia combined with a desire to be simultaneously everywhere and accompanied by an intense envy of human populations that actually possess a culture. The only entity currently on the definitive no-go list for travel or transit is the homeland itself—the great irony of course being that my ease of global movement is thanks largely to a passport bestowed by that very same land.

Indeed, the grotesque privilege of being able to voluntarily uproot oneself—the arbitrary freedom to select a lifestyle of itinerancy—cannot be overstated, particularly in an epoch characterized by mass forced displacement. Much of modern human migration is the result of machinations by none other than my own government—which, in addition to physically dropping bombs on people, is also quite adept at the subtler arts of neoliberal assault. In their book *A Narco History: How the United States and Mexico Jointly Created* the *"Mexican Drug War"*, Mexican novelist Carmen Boullosa and Pulitzer Prize–winning historian Mike Wallace note that, in the aftermath of the passage of the North American Free Trade Agreement (NAFTA) in 1994, the number of Mexican farmers living in poverty increased by one-third, with two million of them eventually forced to abandon their land.[15] And while the bombardment of the Mexican market with subsidized U.S. agricultural exports made a clear mockery of the "F" and "T" in NAFTA, the American annihilation of Mexican livelihoods has never been accepted as a valid reason for U.S.-bound migration. As Jesse A. Myerson writes at *Jacobin Magazine*, "multinational free trade agreements, supranational financial institutions, and transnational corporations ensure that capital can float between nations with all the ease of a monarch butterfly."[16] Cross-border floating by humans without capital, on the other hand, is criminalized.

Somehow, America's established role in screwing over the global populace has not prevented me from regularly encountering a certain refrain abroad—"We hate the American government, but we don't hate the American people"—variations of which I've heard from Colombia to Iran. Never mind hefty U.S. taxpayer contributions to Colombian security forces known for massacring peasants and other civilians under the guise of fighting terror, or the American insistence on reducing the nation of Iran to a swarm of nuclear-obsessed mullahs.[17]

---

15 Boullosa, Carmen and Mike Wallace. *A Narco History: How the United States and Mexico Jointly Created the 'Mexican Drug War.'* New York: OR Books, 2015. Trump, on the other hand, has chosen to once again upend reality by portraying NAFTA as a Mexican plot to destroy the U.S..

16 Myerson, Jesse A. "The Case for Open Borders." *Jacobin Magazine*, 7 March 2013. https://www.jacobinmag.com/2013/03/the-case-for-open-borders

17 Parkin Daniels, Joe. "Colombian army killed thousands more civilians than reported, study claims." *The Guardian*, 8 May 2018. https://www.theguardian.com/world/2018/may/08/colombia-false-positives-scandal-casualties-higher-thought-study. Colombia's "false positives" scandal, first revealed in 2008, saw Colombian troops murder perhaps 10,000 civilians—according to the latest study—and dress up the corpses in guerrilla attire. The false positives were then "used to

Despite this refrain, traveling while American comes with unique baggage. Though there are of course asshole travelers from across the spectrum of nationalities, the assholery of, say, a Paraguayan or Cambodian doesn't carry the same weight as that of an American one, simply because neither Paraguay nor Cambodia is associated with the business of world domination and therefore brattish individual behavior doesn't get interpreted as imperial entitlement writ small. One example off the top of my head: the sexagenarian American visitor to Mexico who once ranted and raved to me about the Mexican media's vilification of Trump, i.e. the creature behind the idea that Mexicans are drug dealers, criminals, rapists, and general bad *hombres*, necessitating an even-more-absurdly-militarized wall on a border that has already caused countless thousands of migrant deaths.[18] My interlocutor did not divulge how he had managed this media analysis without the requisite knowledge of Spanish, although he did introduce himself as "homeless"—by which he meant that he and his wife had various residences at their disposal stateside when they were not availing themselves of the more appealing climes of Mexico and other imperial stomping grounds.

There is no worse caricature of the disproportionately entitled globetrotting élite than the *New York Times* foreign affairs columnist Thomas Friedman. In his book *Longitudes and Attitudes: The World in the Age of Terrorism*, Friedman trumpets his "total freedom, and . . . almost unlimited budget, to explore," as well as his immunity from editorial supervision: "The only

justify U.S. aid military packages while the officers who carried out the executions were rewarded with promotions and time off."

18 Ross, Janell. "From Mexican rapists to bad hombres, the Trump campaign in two moments." The *Washington Post*, 20 October 2016. https://www.washingtonpost.com/news/the-fix/wp/2016/10/20/from-mexican-rapists-to-bad-hombres-the-trump-campaign-in-two-moments/?utm_term=.0767ab104f98.
For migrant deaths, see Miller, Todd. "Over 7,000 Bodies Have Been Found at the U.S.-Mexican Border Since the '90s." *The Nation*, 24 April 2018. https://www.thenation.com/article/over-7000-bodies-have-been-found-at-the-us-mexican-border-since-the-nineties/

person who sees my two columns each week before they show up in the newspaper is a copy editor who edits them for grammar and spelling."[19]

The lack of oversight has enabled Friedman to formulate all sorts of spurious insights over the years, ranging from the theory that McDonald's is the key to world peace, to the notion that Israel's bombing of civilians in Lebanon in 2006 was "not pretty, but it was logical," to the idea that Palestinians suffer from a "collective madness," to the claim that Google Earth and the Beijing Olympics helped fuel the Arab uprisings of 2010–11 (in a masterful response, blogger Sarah Carr suggested some other overlooked causes, such as the 2008 Cheese-Rolling Competition near Gloucester, England)[20].

Among Friedman's favorite things in the world, of course, is the U.S. military. After all, as he explained in 1999: "The hidden hand of the market will never work without a hidden fist—McDonald's cannot flourish without McDonnell Douglas, the builder of the F-15. And the hidden fist that keeps

---

19 Friedman, Thomas. *Longitudes and Attitudes: The World in the Age of Terrorism* (updated subtitle), New York: Anchor Books, 2003 (first Anchor Books edition, newly updated and expanded), p. xiv.

20 Friedman unveiled his "Golden Arches Theory of Conflict Prevention" in *The Lexus and the Olive Tree* (1999). After "Quarter-Pounder[ing]" his "way around the world," he had determined that "no two countries that both had McDonald's had fought a war against each other since each got its McDonald's." That same year, 19 McDonald's-possessing NATO countries happened to go to war against McDonald's-possessing Yugoslavia—and yet all was not lost!, as Friedman determined that Belgrade's capitulation indicated that its citizens "wanted to stand in line for burgers, much more than they wanted to stand in line for Kosovo" (p. 253). I myself have also visited plenty of McDonald's establishments around the world—not for the purpose of ingesting anything but rather because the golden arches for me are the international sign for a free bathroom.
For more about the "not pretty" but "logical" Israeli bombing, see Friedman, Thomas. "Israel's Goals in Gaza?" *New York Times*, 13 January 2009. https://www.nytimes.com/2009/01/14/opinion/14friedman.html; for collectively mad Palestinians, see "War Of Ideas, Part 4." *New York Times*, 18 January 2004. https://www.nytimes.com/2004/01/18/opinion/war-of-ideas-part-4.html; for the lesser known causes of the Arab uprisings, see "This Is Just the Start." *New York Times*, 1 March 2011. https://www.nytimes.com/2011/03/02/opinion/02friedman.html

the world safe for Silicon Valley's technologies is called the United States Army, Air Force, Navy and Marine Corps."[21] Stuff got even more exciting in 2010 when Friedman placed the hidden fist at the vanguard of the green revolution based on the existence of aviation biofuel made from pressed mustard seeds—no small accolade given the Pentagon's continuing distinction as one of the top polluters on the planet.[22]

Following the 2003 invasion of Iraq, Friedman got to play vicarious tough guy on Charlie Rose's TV talk show, where he debuted the argument that American soldiers needed to go "house to house from Basra to Baghdad" with a "very big stick," instructing Iraqis to "Suck. On. This" as punishment for a "terrorism bubble" that was threatening "our open society."[23] The *New York Times* naturally felt no obligation to address its employee's psychopathic demeanor; nor was it ever established what Iraq had to do with the "terrorism bubble" when the nation had supplied zero of the 9/11 hijackers while Friedman's adored Kingdom of Saudi Arabia had supplied 15.[24] In the end, the collective Iraqi blowjob proved a marvelous educa-

---

21 Friedman, Thomas. "A Manifesto for the Fast World." The *New York Times Magazine*, 28 March 1999. https://archive.nytimes.com/www.nytimes.com/books/99/04/25/reviews/friedman-mag.html?_r=1.

22 See Friedman, Thomas. "The U.S.S. Prius." *New York Times*, 18 December 2010. https://www.nytimes.com/2010/12/19/opinion/19friedman.html, and Nazaryan, Alexander. "The U.S. Department of Defense Is One of the World's Biggest Polluters." *Newsweek*, 17 July 2014. https://www.newsweek.com/2014/07/25/us-department-defence-one-worlds-biggest-polluters-259456.html

23 "Thomas Friedman sums up the Iraq war." YouTube: posted by JeremyWBlueDuck37 on 25 January 2011. https://www.youtube.com/watch?v=ZwFaSpca_3Q

24 Over the years, Friedmanian soundbites re: KSA have ranged from "Of course, we must protect the Saudis" ("Playing the Hand We've Dealt." *New York Times*, 20 May 2007 https://www.nytimes.com/2007/05/20/opinion/20friedman.html) to "The problem with Saudi Arabia is not that it has too little democracy. It's that it has too much" ("Hummers Here, Hummers There." *New York Times*, 25 May 2003 https://www.nytimes.com/2003/05/25/opinion/hummers-here-hummers-there.html). When in October 2018 the kingdom murdered Friedman's Saudi journalist pal Jamal Khashoggi in the

tional opportunity for the country's inhabitants, who, Friedman reasoned in 2009, had been exposed to a "melting pot of U.S. soldiers" offering a "million acts of kindness and . . . profound example of how much people of different backgrounds can accomplish when they work together."[25]

To be sure, the pulverization of Iraq was impressive teamwork indeed. Call me cynical, but there are far more profound lessons out there.

Saudi consulate in Istanbul, Friedman was forced to backpedal from his recent ecstatic article "Saudi Arabia's Arab Spring, at Last," an ode to Saudi Crown Prince Mohammed bin Salman (*New York Times*, 23 November 2017.
https://www.nytimes.com/2017/11/23/opinion/saudi-prince-mbs-arab-spring.html).

25 Friedman, Thomas. "Goodbye Iraq, and Good Luck." *New York Times*, 14 July 2009. http://www.nytimes.com/2009/07/15/opinion/15friedman.html.

2. LEBANON

The entrance to the bay of Beirut is magnificent . . . . The town, beautifully situated on a slight eminence, occupies a considerable part of the [south] side of this bay. Beyond the narrow plain of the coast the mountains rise rapidly, and beyond them rises the broad, snow-clad Jebel Sannin . . . . The rosy tint of the mountains contrasting with the deep blue of the sea presents a most picturesque scene by evening light.

This introduction to Beirut appeared in the 1876 Baedeker guide *Palestine and Syria: Handbook for Travellers*—which if nothing else should be of interest to contemporary inhabitants of the world who claim there was never any such thing as Palestine. The guide, excerpted in *A Beirut Anthology: Travel Writing Through the Centuries* (2015), goes on to recommend the cafés near the Beirut customs house as offering the "best opportunity for observing the habits of the native population."[26]

The anthology includes observations by the Frenchman Gérard de Nerval, whose discoveries about natives in nineteenth-century Beirut included that the head ornaments of Druze and Maronite women made them "look like the fabulous unicorns which support the royal arms of England."[27] An

---

26 Gorton, T. J., ed. *A Beirut Anthology: Travel Writing through the Centuries*. Cairo: The American University in Cairo Press, 2015. p. 40.

27 *Ibid.*, p. 106.

excerpt by Gabriel Charmes documents a "picturesque Arab" who looked on as Charmes passed en route from Sidon to Beirut, the landscape growing "steadily more beautiful, and more representative of our preconceived notion of the East than any other." The colors were "more vivid even than the dreams we have while sitting in our European mists," while the whole glorious scene "could have been a corner of Phoenicia, in antiquity."[28]

It's no wonder, then, that Edward Said chose to begin his seminal book *Orientalism* (1978) with a story about a French journalist who, visiting Beirut at the start of the Lebanese civil war in the mid-1970s, "wrote regretfully of the gutted downtown area that 'it had once seemed to belong to . . . the Orient of Chateaubriand and Nerval.'" Indeed, Said said, "the Orient was almost a European invention, and had been since antiquity a place of romance, exotic beings, haunting memories and landscapes"—all of which ultimately contributed to a relationship between Occident and Orient characterized by power, domination, and "varying degrees of a complex hegemony."[29]

Americans, too, quickly mastered Orientalist methods of exoticization, dehumanization, and disempowerment, as well as other handy tricks for facilitating imperial conquest; after all, in strategically valuable areas of the globe, one can't be burdened with natives who fancy themselves in control of their own destinies. Nor did the Lebanese civil war of 1975–90 put a damper on the exotic element. Thomas Friedman, who served as Beirut bureau chief for the *New York Times* in the early 1980s and subsequently penned the bestselling *From Beirut to Jerusalem* (1989), marveled at the manner in which invading Israeli soldiers were thrown for a loop by "the buxom, Cleopatra-eyed Lebanese girls in designer bikinis that left little to

---

28 *Ibid.*, pp. 42–43.

29 Said, Edward. *Orientalism*. New York: Vintage Books (Vintage Books edition), 1979, pp. 1, 5.

the imagination. . . This was not the Sinai, filled with cross-eyed Bedouins and shoeless Egyptian soldiers."[30] Said himself took Friedman to task that same year for "the comic philistinism of [his] ideas," his embrace of "the purest Orientalism," and his peddling of "moronic and hopelessly false dictum[s]."[31]

Nowadays, Beirut has again become something of a darling of the international travel scene, aided by innumerable articles detailing all of the ways to spend money in Lebanon's oh-so-glamorous capital. These reports generally include at least one of the following components:

1. a reference to Beirut as the former "Paris of the Middle East."
2. a reference to Beirut as a "phoenix rising from the ashes."
3. a bout of neo-Orientalist wonder at the mind-blowing juxtaposition of hijabs and mini-skirts, or Hezbollah and billboard lingerie ads.
4. an invented anthropological factoid, such as the *New York Times'* determination that, despite Beirut's many faiths, "at least one religion is universally practiced: sun worship"—particularly at high-end beach clubs where "hordes of heliophiles . . . cultivate their bronzed exteriors"—or *Vogue Magazine*'s revelation that Beirut is now "affectionately referred to as 'Bey.'"[32]

Never mind that no one has ever referred to Beirut as "Bey" outside of a discussion of the city's airport code, or that bronzed exterior cultivation

30 Friedman, Thomas. *From Beirut to Jerusalem*. New York: Farrar, Straus and Giroux, 1991 (first revised edition), p. 131.

31 Edward Said, "The Orientalist Express: Thomas Friedman Wraps Up the Middle East," *Village Voice*, 17 October 1989.

32 "A Weekend in Beirut." *New York Times*, 29 29 April 2010.
https://www.nytimes.com/2010/05/02/travel/02hours.html, and Beckner, Alison. "4 Perfect Days in Beirut. *Vogue*, 13 July 2016 https://www.vogue.com/article/beirut-travel-guide-4-days

isn't exactly compatible with many Lebanese religious persuasions—not to mention the financial obstacles to high-end existence in a country in which the poverty rate in certain areas approaches 65 percent.[33]

Similarly enlightening is the *Times* dispatch on the phenomenon of "women with Louis Vuitton handbags . . . forever extracting their spike heels from the cracks" in the boardwalk at Zaitunay Bay, Beirut's "luxury playground."[34] (Granted, the paper does less damage writing about spike heels than engaging in other activities for which it has been known, e.g. regurgitating Israeli propaganda and preemptively exonerating the IDF for bombing Lebanon to smithereens in any future conflict.[35]) Ditto for

---

33   "Lebanon: North and Akkar Governorates Profile (August 2016)." ReliefWeb, 4 August 2016. https://reliefweb.int/report/lebanon/lebanon-north-and-akkar-governorates-profile-august-2016

34   Barnard, Anne. "Resurgent Beirut Offers Haven Amid Turmoil of Arab Spring." *New York Times*, 13 April 2012. https://www.nytimes.com/2012/04/14/world/middleeast/resurgent-beirut-offers-a-haven-in-the-arab-spring.html

35   See Fernández, Belén. "Turning a south Lebanese village into Israel's next target." *Middle East Eye*, 21 May 2015. https://www.middleeasteye.net/essays/militarised-journalism-turns-lebanese-village-israel-s-next-target-1498733793 In which I suggest that the *Times* cease trying to make a buck off of subscriptions and instead start invoicing the Israeli military for PR services. In a 13 May 2015 article datelined Tel Aviv, "Israel Says Hezbollah Positions Put Lebanese at Risk" (https://www.nytimes.com/2015/05/13/world/middleeast/israel-says-hezbollah-positions-put-lebanese-at-risk.html?referrer&_r=1), Isabel Kershner faithfully relayed the IDF's determination that south Lebanon was so awash in Hezbollah that, for example, the miniscule village of Muhaybib contained no fewer than "nine arms depots, five rocket-launching sites, four infantry positions, signs of three underground tunnels, three anti-tank positions and, in the very center of the village, a Hezbollah command post." The village of Shaqra, population 4,000, was meanwhile home to "about 400 military sites and facilities belonging to Hezbollah." The article specifies that the *Times'* Anne Barnard, author of the aforementioned investigation into Louis Vuitton handbags and spike heels, "contributed reporting from Beirut"—although it's unclear why she couldn't have made the two-hour drive to the villages in question for a quick glance around. I myself, though in possession of a budget nowhere comparable to that of the *Times*, managed to rent a cheap car and visit both villages, where I did not see any Hezbollah command posts but did see plenty of schoolchildren, old people, houses, farms, a colorful establishment offering "Botox filling," a place called Magic Land, a painting of Che Guevara, and a graffito reading "THUG LIFE."

VICE's predictable contribution to the study of Lebanese culture, "Fighting for the Right to Party in Beirut," in which we learn about a revolutionary arrangement whereby "bars offer coke-fueled benders down the street from Hezbollah headquarters."[36]

Of course, the glorification of élite excess is nothing new in a global panorama in which shameless and all-encompassing materialism directly serves the interests of the powers that be. It is in this context that we must view the encouragement and applause for Arab populations sufficiently trained in Western-style decadence so as not to pose too much of a threat to the world order. In the case of Lebanon in particular, gleeful Orientalist convulsions over the Beirut "renaissance" and the idea that the Lebanese are so much "like us" invalidate and delegitimize the aspirations of those in Lebanon with potentially more pressing objectives than coke-fueled benders—like, say, the right not to be occupied and killed by Israel. Naturally, anyone putting up resistance to U.S.-Israeli designs in the region is potentially guilty of sabotaging Lebanon's "Paris of the Middle East" identity in favor of the alternative "terrorist hotbed" narrative.

One such saboteur is a Palestinian-Lebanese man called Hassan whom I once happened to marry as part of a heavily wine-fueled scheme to procure for him a U.S. passport, with which document he might travel to Israel to see his late father's Palestinian family members in a village near Nazareth. His father had fled his birthplace as a child in 1948 when the state of Israel undertook to erect itself on Palestinian land, eliminating more than 400 villages, killing some 10,000 Palestinians, and expelling

---

36 Von Aue, Mary. "Fighting for the Right to Party in Beirut." *VICE*, 3 October 2014. https://www .vice.com/en_us/article/qbenvq/fighting-for-the-right-to-party-in-beirut One would expect nothing less from *VICE*, but the effective elevation of coke-fueled benders to the status of noble resistance against injustice makes a mockery of the very real struggles of the average non-élite Lebanese.

three-quarters of a million more.[37] Taken in by a south Lebanese family, he later married a Lebanese Shia from the southern village of Shehabieh; Lebanon's identity laws being what they are, however, Hassan is permanently categorized as a Sunni Palestinian refugee, with citizenship, basic rights, and job opportunities curtailed accordingly. This despite his previous service in Lebanon's primarily Shia Amal Movement, in which capacity he participated in the struggle to liberate Lebanese territory from Israeli occupation.

Given Israel's unilateral criminalization of any suggestion of a Palestinian right of return, Hassan is essentially doubly deprived of a homeland, on both his mother's and father's sides. Back in 2008, the situation got us to thinking that the least my own repudiated homeland could do in compensation for its annual multibillion-dollar donations to Israel would be to provide him with the passport necessary to allow Hassan to reconnect with his Palestinian past just south of the Lebanese border.[38]

Our wine-induced disregard for the numerous hurdles to this matrimonial scheme meant that Hassan and I never made it so far as to register our union at the U.S. embassy-fortress north of Beirut, although we did at least eventually succeed in navigating Lebanon's sectarian bureaucracy, resulting in my inscription as wife number one on Hassan's Palestinian identity card. Meanwhile, Hassan served as benevolent guide to picturesque

---

37 See Black, Ian. "Remembering the Nakba: Israeli group puts 1948 Palestine back on the map." *The Guardian*, 2 May 2014. https://www.theguardian.com/world/2014/may/02/nakba-israel-palestine-zochrot-history

38 Since then, U.S. financial commitments to Israel have only expanded. See, for example, "Key U.S. lawmakers want to boost Israel's $38 billion defense aid package." *Reuters*, 28 February 2018. https://www.reuters.com/article/us-usa-israel-defense/key-u-s-lawmakers-want-to-boost-israels-38-billion-defense-aid-package-idUSKCN1GB2NQ

scenery and native habits, and did his damnedest to make me feel at home in a land where he most certainly wasn't.

*   *   *

Amelia and I first met Hassan while hitchhiking in Lebanon shortly after Israel's 2006 assault—not to be confused with Israel's 1978, 1982, 1993, or 1996 assaults, or its 22-year occupation of the southern part of the country.

Setting out from southwestern Turkey in early September, we had hitchhiked east for 1,000 or so kilometers to the Syrian border, a smooth journey apart from a few instances in which we were presumed to be Russian prostitutes despite our best efforts to clad ourselves in Turkish farming attire.

As a U.S. citizen, I was not technically permitted to obtain a Syrian visa on the border—neither was Amelia, although she had the benefit of not hailing from a country that had designated Syria part of the expanded Axis of Evil—but a mere five-hour wait produced the desired slew of multicolored stamps, markings across various passport pages, and sticker specifying that "WHEN HE WANTS TO STAY MORE THAN 15 DAYS HE MUST REFER TO THE BRANCH OF IMMIGRATION." While certain acquaintances we acquired in Syria requested that we not pronounce the name of President Bashar al-Assad in anything above a whisper, Amelia and I did appreciate various other freedoms, as when a shopkeeper in the coastal city of Tartus assured us it was no problem whatsoever—and would in fact be downright spectacular—if we were to sit in the middle of the sidewalk and drink beer.

Crossing over from Syria into Lebanon, we were plied with copious amounts of orange soda by the border guards on the Syrian side, who then halted a passing vehicle and commanded the driver to transport us as far as Beirut—a trajectory rendered lengthier by Israel's recent bombing of bridges and roads. The bombed bridges, however, did not prepare us for the sight of the flattened neighborhoods in Beirut's southern suburbs or the razed villages of the country's south. As the prominent Lebanese novelist Elias Khoury wrote that same month in an essay titled "Meditations upon Destruction," which was translated into English in *The War on Lebanon: A Reader*: "It is devastation. It is a pure devastation that is like nothing you have ever seen—apart from devastation. Ruins stretching to the horizon, challenging the sky. Stars trembling, and so also are people's eyes. Everything is tremulous and shimmering, everything is in suspension."[39] Indeed, when Amelia and I left Lebanon some months later, the rubble had become so familiar that intact structures had begun to appear disfigured and out of place.

Our inaugural encounter with Hassan took place in the south Lebanese city of Tyre, former stomping ground of Alexander the Great as well as other more contemporary invaders. Amelia and I were in the process of hitchhiking for the second time to the border town of Bint Jbeil, a.k.a. the "capital of the Resistance" and site of a fierce battle that summer, where we had recently met a family with three children—all of them U.S. citizens—who had returned from a long-term stint in Michigan just in time for the hostilities. The family had spent ten days packed into a room with dozens of other people under Israeli bombardment and had then fled north in a convoy of cars, the last of which was eliminated by airstrike. America, for its part, had initially attempted to charge U.S. passport holders out the ass for the luxury of evacuation, as saving your own people is apparently more of a financial burden than rush-shipping bombs to Israel.[40]

---

39 Hovsepian, Nubar and Rashid Khalidi. *The War on Lebanon: A Reader*. Northampton, MA: Olive Branch Press, 2007.

40 Neuman, Johanna and Peter Spiegel. "Pay-as-You-Go Evacuation Roils Capitol Hill." *Los Angeles Times*, 19 July 2006. http://articles.latimes.com/2006/jul/19/world/fg-repay19

Hassan and his companion Mo—short for Mohammad—were both in their early thirties. They had a Range Rover and a stockpile of alcoholic beverages, and they pledged to escort us from Tyre to Bint Jbeil. Halfway there, the plan unraveled and we found ourselves instead bound for a bar in Beirut where the pair professed to have business to handle. Acquainted for less than a year, Hassan and Mo had jointly established a car rental company in Tyre that appeared to be structured loosely around the rental concept and to additionally specialize in blackmail and detective-type services.

On the ride north it was revealed that the reason Mo attached the term "innit" to the end of every sentence was that he had temporarily exiled himself to the UK following south Lebanon's liberation from Israeli occupation in May 2000. This had seemed the wisest move, he said, on account of his service in Israel's proxy South Lebanon Army (SLA), which had been tasked with torturing and otherwise antagonizing sectors of the south Lebanese population who were suspected of being insufficiently enthusiastic about Israel's regional ambitions.[41] His claim that SLA duty had been a result not of personal preference but of threats to his family members and property had not prevented him from being thrown in jail when he returned to Lebanon—or from being affectionately referred to by Hassan as "The Betrayer."

Hassan's own armed history with the Amal Movement—the domain of civil warlord-turned-eternal Lebanese Parliament Speaker Nabih

---

41 See Porter, Lizzie. "A legacy of torture: Inside Lebanon's Khiam jail." *Al Jazeera*, 14 August 2017. https://www.aljazeera.com/indepth/features/2017/08/legacy-torture-lebanon-khiam-jail-170813125414823.html. The notorious SLA prison-cum-torture center in Khiam, south Lebanon, was converted into a museum and memorial following the Israeli withdrawal in 2000—and then it was bombed by the Israelis in 2006. They also killed four UN observers stationed in the town (McCarthy, Rory and Suzanne Goldberg and Oliver Burkeman, "Israelis ignored repeated warnings before killing UN observers." *The Guardian*, 27 July 2006. https://www.theguardian.com/world/2006/jul/27/syria.israel4)

Berri—commenced in the 1990s after the conclusion of the 15-year civil war, during which Amal had intermittently fought the Palestinians along with other fluctuating nemeses. While Mo was busy engaging in treason, Hassan said, he had dedicated himself wholeheartedly to the Hezbollah-led struggle against the Israeli occupation, even preparing a martyr photo of himself in the event of elimination in the line of duty. When liberation finally arrived, however, he sought compensation from Amal for a jeep incinerated by the Israelis and was pointedly reminded that he was Palestinian and not Lebanese.

That was the end of that relationship and the onset of Hassan's loathing for Berri, who, like others in the Lebanese ruling class, has finagled his own territorial occupation of sorts in the form of lucrative fiefdoms and shameless self-portraits that saturate corresponding sectarian geographies. Berri's Beirut uber-residence enjoys a security perimeter that encompasses an ever-changing number of city blocks and adds to the travails of the Beirut pedestrian, who already has to contend with the near-total lack of space for the average human among buildings, cars, and politicians. Hassan nonetheless professed a profound admiration for Hezbollah leader Hassan Nasrallah, whom he considered a man of principle and thus an anomaly on the Lebanese political scene.

The Range Rover's progress toward Beirut was interrupted several times by bombed-out sections of road and once by a throng of policemen, who said nothing about the fact that we had been traveling at the speed of light or that the car was full of beer bottles and instead waved us on our way, enabling Hassan to continue narrating his autobiography. He hoped to one day compile these anecdotes into a full-length manuscript, tentatively titled *Life of Hassan*.

Following the break with Amal, Hassan had surveyed his options in Lebanon, where Palestinians are banned from a long list of professions, property ownership, and anything else that might solidify their presence in the country where they have now spent more than seven decades—many of them in squalid camps.[42] The reason Palestinians must be deprived of rights at all cost has to do with Lebanon's confessional system, in which individuals are forcibly categorized by religious sect and political and administrative posts are allocated according to the ostensible size of each religious community. The post of President is reserved exclusively for a Maronite Christian, Prime Minister for a Sunni Muslim, and Parliament Speaker for a Shia.[43] Never mind that the last national census was conducted in 1932, when Lebanon existed under the charitable tutelage of the Maronite-favoring French.

United in their efforts to royally screw over the masses, the current Lebanese élite are more than happy to stoke sectarian divisions in order

---

42 See, for example, Cassel, Matthew. "Palestinians in Lebanon demonstrate for their rights." *The Electronic Intifada*, 29 June 2010. https://electronicintifada.net/content/palestinians-lebanon-demonstrate-their-rights/8896

43 With the influx into Lebanon of more than one million Syrian refugees following the onset of the Syrian war in 2011, Lebanon acquired loads more people to deprive of rights, many of whom were forced to take up residence in dismal tent settlements that offered little protection from the elements. In 2016, I visited one such settlement in Lebanon's Bekaa Valley that was literally located in a landfill. Syrian-specific curfews were enforced in some areas, and abuse and discrimination against these refugees has been well documented. While it's certainly true that Lebanon—a tiny country already suffering from aging and ineffective infrastructure and a dearth of services—shouldn't be required to take responsibility for a disproportionate number of refugees, particularly when the U.S. almost entirely exempts itself from the refugee "burden" despite continuing to fuel conflict in the Middle East, the Lebanese government's self-victimization (when there is a government) is also disingenuous. The fact of the matter is that, Palestinian and Syrian refugees aside, the Lebanese state doesn't do jack shit for the majority of its own population—some of whom have been known to contend with a mere two hours of government electricity per day, not to mention the near-total lack of affordable health care options or other basic needs. The upshot, in the end, is that refugees provide a convenient scapegoat for the government's own willful failures vis-à-vis the Lebanese. (See Fernández, Belén. "Syrian refugees in Lebanon: Whose breaking point?" *Middle East Eye*, 13 October 2015. https://www.middleeasteye.net/columns/syrian-refugees-lebanon-whose-breaking-point-1832663622)

to preclude the emergence of any sort of pan-sectarian cohesiveness and solidarity that might pose a threat to their profitable stranglehold on power. Lebanese leaders are well aware that dominance and riches are facilitated by popular oppression—and that keeping people poor and divided automatically renders them dependent on the leaders themselves for survival. The moral of the story for Palestinians in Lebanon is that any suggestion of citizenship and civil rights is regarded as an unacceptable assault on the status quo, since this would officially add a whole lot of Sunni Muslims to the mix. In light of the inhospitable arrangement, Hassan had concluded that his best bet was to attempt to relocate to Europe, and in 2001 he traveled to Istanbul, where a Turkish mafia ring promised him passage to Greece for $1,000.

Thus began an odyssey of sorts that saw Hassan packed into the back of a frozen-goods truck with a crowd of people and no air. After surviving near asphyxiation, he was put on a boat that broke down 100 meters off the Turkish coast, followed by a boat that sank and finally a boat that deposited Hassan and his fellow voyagers at some other location in Turkey, which they were told was Greece—a claim that was presumably easily debunked thanks to Turkey's infatuation with its own flag. Tired of repeated run-ins with Turkish law enforcement, Hassan returned by bus to Lebanon, which then served as a launching pad for subsequent chapters of *Life of Hassan*, including "Hassan Goes to Kiev"—in which he was apprehended by a Ukrainian police dog while trudging through the snow toward Poland— and "Hassan Goes to Madrid," in which he spent five days in Madrid's Barajas airport looking for a loophole in the passport control process.

When the Spaniards eventually took notice of him and wanted to know why his connecting flight to Cuba—one of the few places in the world that welcomes the Lebanese travel document for Palestinian refugees— had departed without him five days earlier, he fabricated a dramatic alibi involving a desperate and sleepless search for a lost handbag. The airport security personnel were, he said, moved by his tale of woe, and treated him to an extravagant feast before putting him on the plane back to Beirut.

Resigning himself to immobility for the time being, Hassan opened an internet café, in the name of his Lebanese niece, in front of his mother's house in the south Lebanese village of Shehabieh. Hassan's father had passed away years before, never returning to Palestine since fleeing to Lebanon on foot in 1948. Hassan had also lost three sisters, who had been killed by Israel, a sniper, and a car, respectively. Any effective operation of the internet café was thwarted by the perennial lack of electricity in Lebanon, but Hassan found activities to keep himself busy on the side, and when Israel attacked in 2006 he assisted in the northward evacuation of his family members and neighbors.

Amelia and I tagged along on a few more Hassan-Mo activities prior to departing Lebanon, such as the high-speed running of unspecified errands in the rubble of Dahiyeh, Beirut's southern suburbs—or the "Hezbollah stronghold," if you prefer the reductionist and carnage-abetting lexicon of the mainstream media.[44] The radio volume was lowered only long enough for the recounting of another past Hassanian misadventure: "Hassan Is Tied to an Interrogation Chair in Dahiyeh."

When it came time for us to hitchhike back to Turkey, Hassan and Mo volunteered to deposit us back at the Syrian border, stopping at a roadside bazaar along the way so that Hassan could procure for us oversized and unflattering apparel meant to guard against any repeat of the Russian

---

44 Whether for lack of imagination or for reasons more sinister, the media is often incapable of describing Dahiyeh sans the "stronghold" descriptor. This designation apparently explains everything that happens there, including ISIS suicide bombings. Never mind that A) Hezbollah is a political party in Lebanon with widespread civilian support, and B) Dahiyeh is not monolithically Hezbollah but rather composed of people of varying political and religious persuasions.

prostitute diagnosis. Also accompanying us on the return trip was the mound of possessions we had accumulated in Lebanon, among them a gigantic Hezbollah wall clock gifted to us by a veteran of the recent conflict who had picked us up hitchhiking in the south and taken us on a tour of what remained of his house.

Speaking of clocks, IDF Chief of Staff Dan Halutz had recently proclaimed Israel's goal to "turn back the clock in Lebanon by 20 years," which would have put the country in about 1986, the heyday of the Israeli occupation and four years after the Israeli terror-spree in Lebanon that killed some 20,000 people, the vast majority of them civilians. This invasion, incidentally, was what gave rise to Hezbollah in the first place.[45] The U.S., on the other hand, had sponsored a more forward-looking outlook in 2006, with Secretary of State Condoleezza Rice designating Israel's summer onslaught the "birth pangs of a new Middle East"—an impressive analogy given that the goal of the birthing process is not generally to kill the baby.[46] George W. Bush, meanwhile, had offered the sophisticated mid-conflict assessment that Syria simply needed "to get Hezbollah to stop doing this shit and it's all over," a prescription that conveniently overlooked the role of the party with the monopoly on shit-doing in the region.[47]

* * *

---

45 "Hezbollah warns Israel over raids." *BBC News*, 12 July 2006. http://news.bbc.co.uk/2/hi/middle_east/5173078.stm

46 "Secretary Rice Holds a News Conference." *Washington Post*, 21 July 2006. http://www.washingtonpost.com/wp-dyn/content/article/2006/07/21/AR2006072100889.html While the birthing metaphor is fittingly Orientalist, it's not clear what role Rice herself has been assigned in the obstetric miracle. Homicidal midwife, perhaps?

47 "Transcript: Bush and Blair's unguarded chat." *BBC News*, 18 July 2006. http://news.bbc.co.uk/2/hi/5188258.stm. This assessment was put forth in a conversation at the G8 conference in Russia with UK prime minister Tony Blair, whom Bush addressed as "Yo, Blair." Prior to the pair's discovery that an overlooked microphone was recording their banter, other important international

I next saw Hassan in 2008, when I traveled by bus from Turkey to Syria and was once again granted a Syrian visa after an unnecessary quantity of tea with the border guards. Hassan, who had since parted ways with Mo, retrieved me from the Syrian frontier and supplied me with sleeping accommodations on the floor of his mother's living room in Shehabieh, under a portrait of his father and a painting of Shia Islam's revered martyr Imam Hussein. On luckier days, I was also supplied with servings of his mother's green beans.

Hassan was engaged in his usual assortment of entrepreneurial endeavors, ranging from collaboration in a friend's scheme to sell a nonexistent diamond to a German aristocrat to collaboration in a larger scheme to facilitate Iraqi migration to Europe. Although never quite successful, this operation theoretically involved shipping Iraqis from Lebanon to Venezuela, where they would then obtain Venezuelan passports and proceed to the Old Continent—thereby confirming the pivotal role of the Bolivarian Republic, obsessively vilified by U.S. neocons, in global terrorist operations like assisting refugees from countries destroyed by the U.S.

Hassan had also been in increasingly frequent contact with his father's family near Nazareth, who assured him that his Palestinian roots were alive and well and that they were holding onto a plot of land for him—if only he could find a way to get there. Hence Hassan's latest ambition to marry a European passport holder in order to one day acquire a passport himself with which he then might be permitted entry into Israel.

At the time of my arrival in May, however, Hassan's primary activity consisted of driving back and forth across Lebanon, a country smaller than

matters were also addressed, such as Blair's gift to Bush of a sweater he claimed to have knitted himself.

Connecticut, as the constant motion apparently helped to alleviate the claustrophobia of imposed borders. The illusion of freedom was no doubt bolstered by the dearth of traffic laws. A cassette tape of Enigma had been appointed endless soundtrack to the directionless journey, for which I was granted the passenger seat.

The ride became briefly smoother when four days after I got to Lebanon the country descended into a deadly mini civil war pitting Hezbollah, Amal, and their allies against Western-backed pro-government forces and resulting in a self-imposed curfew of sorts thanks to which Hassan and I were able to park the car in the middle of the highway and smoke cigarettes. Complications then arose in the form of impromptu checkpoints, as when an enraged crowd of Druze men encircled Hassan's car and demanded his sectarian orientation—"Sunni or Shia?"—a more than slightly uncomfortable reminder of the ID card–based checkpoint killings of the civil war. In this case, Hassan's Lebanese travel document for Palestinian refugees automatically classified him as Sunni and saved the day, in perhaps the first recorded instance of said document's utility in the history of the world.

Things eventually settled down, traffic returned to normal, and we continued our restless movement, careening through the mountains of the north and the valleys of south Lebanon. Hassan knew the latter terrain intimately from his days as a militant, and the landscape would often elicit more tales from *Life of Hassan*, such as the time he hid from Israel in a certain garden or the time he arrived in the village of Qana in 1996 to find that the Israeli military had slaughtered more than 100 civilians sheltering at a United Nations compound. On other occasions, he would declare himself tired of remembering and tired even of Palestine, and would accelerate in the direction of oblivion.

Palestine was, however, impossible to forget given its continuous presence—and not only on south Lebanese road signs pointing in English to

"Palastain." Sitting by the sea in Tyre at night, Hassan and I would watch as Israel flickered just beyond the gleaming border fortress belonging to UNIFIL, the UN's alleged "interim force" in Lebanon, which since its establishment in 1978 has done nothing to defend the country, preferring instead to engage in heavily armed shopping expeditions.

One afternoon in the Lebanese border town of Kfar Kila—where Edward Said famously threw a stone at Israel—Hassan performed his own symbolic cross-border gesture in the form of an extended middle finger to the Israeli soldiers parked just across the fence, while I exhibited great bravery by yelping and endeavoring to sink into the floormat. Nor could Palestine be unremembered in the Beirut Palestinian refugee camps of Sabra and Shatila, where Israeli-backed right-wing Lebanese Christian Phalangists massacred up to several thousand civilians over the course of three days in 1982 and where Hassan sometimes purchased vegetables.[48]

This Israeli-Lebanese alliance was curious, to say the least, since, as veteran Middle East journalist Robert Fisk has pointed out, the founder of the Phalangists got the idea for his party from none other than the Nazis.[49]

---

48 There are varying estimates as to the number of fatalities. For an estimate of 1,700, see Fisk, Robert. "The forgotten massacre." *The Independent*. 15 September 2012. https://www.independent.co.uk/news/world/middle-east/the-forgotten-massacre-8139930.html. For an estimate of 800-3,500, see "1982: Refugees massacred in Beirut camps." *BBC* website. http://news.bbc.co.uk/onthisday/hi/dates/stories/september/17/newsid_2519000/2519637.stm

49 Fisk, Robert. "Gemayel's mourners know that in Lebanon nothing is what it seems." *The Independent*, 23 November 2006. https://www.independent.co.uk/voices/commentators/fisk/robert-fisk-gemayels-mourners-know-that-in-lebanon-nothing-is-what-it-seems-425427.html. And yet fascism, it seems, can build all sorts of bridges. Just recall a certain letter—published in the *New York Times* in 1948 shortly after the establishment of the state of Israel and signed by Albert Einsten, Hannah Arendt, and other prominent Jews—denouncing the Israeli Herut party, led by Menachem Begin, for being "closely akin in its organization, methods, political philosophy and social appeal to the Nazi and Fascist parties" (see Schuster, Ruth. "1948: N.Y. Times Publishes Letter by Einstein, Other Jews Accusing Menachem Begin of Fascism." *Haaretz*, 4 December 2014. https://www.haaretz.com/jewish/.premium-1948-n-y-times-letter-by-einstein-slams-begin-1.5340057).

Charmingly, Phalangist iconography still dominates certain sectarian districts in Lebanon. The prominent Beirut neighborhood of Ashrafieh, for example, plays host to a statue of a kneeling figure mid-fascist salute—yet another indication of the exclusivity of space in Lebanon and of competing visions of homeland.

When Hassan resumed strategizing about taking an arbitrary European bride, a surplus of wine one evening propelled us to the sudden conclusion that it would be far easier for him to marry me. And so it was that we soon found ourselves in the south Lebanese office of a jolly Shia sheikh, who chortled at Hassan's suggestion that a premarital virginity test be conducted in the adjoining room, protesting that there were far too many filing cabinets in the way.

Getting married was a breeze. Registering the marriage, however, was another matter altogether, as we learned from weeks of shuttling between various Lebanese and Palestinian authorities, including one building Hassan dubbed the "Office of Stupid People." The upshot was that a Palestinian male could not be married by a Shia sheikh unless he had specifically converted to Shiism and was marked as having done so on relevant documents.

This obstacle, too, was ultimately overcome—albeit not until shortly after I had departed Lebanon and shortly before Hassan was admitted to Lebanon's notorious Roumieh prison for two years for a scheme involving large quantities of fake cement and a fake Somali ambassador. At some point during his internment I sent him a letter from Argentina, in which I

Later, as prime minister of Israel, Begin oversaw the 1978 and 1982 invasions of Lebanon. It was this latter invasion which featured the productive collaboration between Israeli forces and Lebanese Phalangists.

happened to mention a television report I had done re: the visit to Buenos Aires of maleficent Israeli foreign minister Avigdor Lieberman. The officials at Roumich, having already established that Hassan regularly placed phone calls to the Zionist entity (read: his father's Palestinian family members), zeroed in on the word "Israel" in my letter and deduced that Hassan was a spy, whereupon he was carted off to an underground cell and blindfolded for five days. When I later spoke to him, he would give me no other details of the experience aside from the fact that he would have preferred to die.

Preparing myself for karmic retribution, I returned to Lebanon in 2010, but merely had my passport confiscated upon arrival and was ordered to Lebanese General Security headquarters to collect it. There I was interrogated for four hours on subjects ranging from whether or not I liked Israel to whether Israel or Hezbollah had emerged victorious from the 2006 war to why I held my pen incorrectly. When the interrogation took a sharp turn toward a discussion of Iraqis immigrating to Europe, it became clear that my name had come up in the course of some investigation into that particular Hassanian mission. Unbeknownst to me, a friend waiting outside phoned the U.S. embassy to intervene on my behalf, at which point my passport was restored and I was free to visit Hassan at his place of imprisonment.

One sunny morning, Hassan's sister and I drove north from Beirut to Roumieh, where amenities in recent years have included egregiously overcrowded cells, torture-happy representatives of the state, and a unique arrangement that effectively permitted Salafi-jihadist prisoners to rule an entire section of the complex largely off-limits to prison guards.[50]

---

50 See "Lebanon: Monitor Detention to Combat Torture." Human Rights Watch, 26 June 2015. https://www.hrw.org/news/2015/06/26/lebanon-monitor-detention-combat-torture,

During my brief reunion with Hassan, for which the guards allowed him to emerge for a few moments into the sunlight, he assured me that he was collecting all sorts of stories for *Life of Hassan* and presented me with some beaded deodorant canisters and other arts and crafts he had produced. I saw him again in 2012 following his release from Roumieh, when he explained to me that he had been recruited to assist with bus tours in Lebanon for citizens of Iraq interested in learning about the perks of democracy and good governance—a ludicrous premise given Lebanon's modus operandi, he acknowledged, but anyway better than jail.

A subsequent 2016 rendezvous at a Syrian restaurant in Beirut revealed that Hassan had tired of the bus-tour gig but had grand plans for the launch of a Shia resistance in Palestine. The colossal matter of logistics aside, there's no denying that—as the U.S. insists on subsidizing Israel's habitual obliteration of Palestinians while endorsing its ever more apocalyptic threats against Lebanon—a whole lot of resistance is in order.

and Fernández, Belén. "The raid on Roumieh, Lebanon's prison-state." *Middle East Eye*, 24 January 2015. https://www.middleeasteye.net/columns/raid-roumieh-lebanon-s-prison-state-1331411396

3. HONDURAS

In the predawn hours of June 28, 2009, heavily armed Honduran soldiers descended upon the Tegucigalpa residence of the nation's president, Manuel (Mel) Zelaya, and carted him off to Costa Rica in his pajamas, never again to be restored to his lawful post.

Ever so slightly left-leaning, Zelaya had stepped on the toes of the entrenched Honduran oligarchy, whose members had long ago pledged allegiance to the predatory capitalism endorsed by their benefactors in the United States. Not only had Zelaya raised the monthly urban and rural minimum wages to a whopping $290 and $213, respectively, he had also shown himself to be more willing than his predecessors to listen to the complaints of impoverished communities affected by mining and other toxic operations by international corporations. All of this naturally indicated that the communist apocalypse was nigh.

The last straw came in the form a nonbinding public opinion survey, scheduled for June 28, in which citizens would be asked whether or not they supported the inclusion of an extra ballot box at upcoming elections in order to then vote on whether or not to convene a constituent assembly to update the national constitution. As the Honduran right-wing and concerned gringos spun it, this was concrete proof that Zelaya was scheming to abolish the constitutional article that limited presidents to a single term and to thereby install himself as eternal dictator.[51] Of no consequence, apparently, was that any constitutional tweaking would only take place after Zelaya had already left power. Eventually, the article in question was abolished anyway, albeit under a sufficiently ultra-rightist administration so as not to merit a peep from the guardians of democracy.

In the months following Zelaya's pajama-clad expatriation, the U.S. busied itself hemming and hawing over how to categorize his ouster without resorting to the obvious descriptor—"military coup"—that would then trigger massive cutoffs in aid to the post-Zelaya allies. After initially declaring that the U.S. was "withholding any formal legal determination" regarding the Coup-Type Thing in Honduras, Secretary of State Hillary Clinton set about "strategiz[ing] on a plan to restore order in [the country] and ensure that free and fair elections could be held quickly and legitimately, which would render the question of Zelaya moot and give the Honduran people a chance to choose their own future."[52]

---

51 In an op-ed for the *Wall Street Journal*, Lanny Davis took the liberty of asserting that Zelaya had aimed to "declare himself president ad infinitum"—which was actually categorically impossible given that the proposed extra ballot box was to accompany the very same elections in which Zelaya himself was ineligible to run, having already served his allotted single term ("The Way Forward in Honduras," 9 November 2009. https://www.wsj.com/articles/SB10001424052748704402404574525693251573708). Davis, an old law school buddy of Hillary Clinton's and former special counsel to Bill Clinton, was hired in the aftermath of the coup by the Latin American Business Council of Honduras to lobby on Capitol Hill on behalf of the *golpistas*. Leaked emails revealed that Davis—who would later help organize a Ready for Hillary fundraiser in the suburbs of DC in 2014—was also suggested by Secretary of State Clinton as a back-channel liaison to the illegitimate Honduran coup president Roberto Micheletti.

52 For the withholding, see Aroon, Preeti. "Clinton: It's a coup, but not officially." *Foreign Policy*, 30 June 2009. https://foreignpolicy.com/2009/06/30/clinton-its-a-coup-but-not-officially/ For the rendering moot of Zelaya, see Clinton, Hillary. *Hard Choices*. New York: Simon and Schuster, 2014, p. 266.

This, at least, is what she herself told us in her 2014 memoir *Hard Choices*, in a passage mysteriously excised from the paperback edition the following year.[53] New elections were indeed swiftly held, and mootness rendered— although it's anyone's guess as to how elections staged after an illegal coup could qualify as legitimate, particularly when the Honduran people had already chosen Zelaya to serve out his four-year term.

Not that the U.S. has ever been overly keen on permitting the public in Honduras—or anywhere in America's self-declared "backyard," for that matter—jurisdiction over its own future. The Contra war of the 1980s comes to mind, when the affectionate moniker "USS Honduras" was bestowed on the Banana-republic-cum-launchpad for U.S. proxy forces assaulting Nicaragua, a nation that had veered from the straight and narrow path of obsequiousness to the big northern boss. In a 1986 essay, famed Uruguayan writer Eduardo Galeano observed that Ronald Reagan's "demonization" of Nicaragua served to "justify the U.S. war economy." Paraphrasing a suggestion from Sandinista leader Tomás Borge that pretty soon Nicaragua would also be held responsible for AIDS as well as the devaluation of the dollar, Galeano pointed out the irony in the fact that the nation claiming that "even the stars must be militarized . . . to confront the terrorist threat" was the same one engaged in "terrorist acts against Nicaragua, practicing terrorism as an imperial right and . . . exporting state terrorism, on an industrial scale, under the registered trademark of the National Security Doctrine."[54]

---

53 For the new-and-improved, clean version of the book, see Clinton, Hillary. *Hard Choices*. New York: Simon and Schuster Paperbacks, 2015. I discovered this disappearing act while researching an essay for the following collection: Featherstone, Liza, ed. *False Choices: The Faux Feminism of Hillary Rodham Clinton*. New York: Verso, 2016.

54 For the original Spanish, see Galeano, Eduardo. "Defensa de Nicaragua." *El País*, 26 November 1986. https://elpais.com/diario/1986/11/26/internacional/533343610_850215.html

Nor was U.S. National Security in short supply in Honduras, where, as the *Baltimore Sun* reported in 1995, a CIA-trained élite death squad by the name of Battalion 316 had "stalked, kidnapped, tortured and murdered hundreds of Honduran men and women"—in short, "terrorized Honduras for much of the 1980s" on behalf of the U.S. war on communism.[55] Other U.S. exploits of the Contra period included collaboration with top Honduran drug lord Juan Ramón Matta Ballesteros, whose airline SETCO was, Roxanne Dunbar-Ortiz notes in her Contra war memoir *Blood on the Border*, known as the "CIA airline."[56] To be sure, factoids like these greatly boost the U.S. government's credibility in waging its interminable war on drugs.

When I arrived to Tegucigalpa exactly a month after the 2009 coup, Honduran men and women had once again found themselves in the crosshairs, as daily and almost exasperatingly peaceful anti-coup marches were routinely met with maniacal opposition by Honduran soldiers and police. At the beginning of July, for example, Honduran teenager Isis Obed Murillo had been fatally shot in the head by security forces at a pro-Zelaya rally. A schoolteacher was shot at a subsequent demonstration, also fatally and in the head, after which the prominent Honduran newspaper *El Heraldo* obediently explained that the man "had abandoned his classroom in order to go out and protest in the streets," in case there was any doubt about who was to blame for his murder.

I had traveled to Tegucigalpa from Argentina, where I was visiting my parents following a four-month hitchhiking excursion with Amelia through Ecuador, Colombia, and Venezuela. Knowing approximately nothing about Honduras—part of my brain had even assumed it was an island—I

---

55 Thompson, Ginger and Gary Cohn. "Torturers' confessions." *The Baltimore Sun*, 13 June 1995. https://www.baltimoresun.com/news/maryland/bal-negroponte2-story.html#page=1

56 Dunbar-Ortiz, Roxanne. *Blood on the Border: A Memoir of the Contra War*. Norman: University of Oklahoma Press, 2016, p. 233

nonetheless decided that the Central American nation was as good a place as any to postpone sorting out my life. In the process, I became ever more acquainted with my homeland's own intimate role in fucking over other people's homelands.

Obviously, traveling to Honduras as a U.S. citizen was quite a bit easier than the inverse scenario, as Hondurans who have risked their existence journeying to the U.S. border can testify. I was also, of course, able to extricate myself from the country at will—no small luxury in the postcoup era of near-total impunity, when Honduras maintained the distinction of being the homicide capital of the world.[57]

My initial accommodations were an $8-per-night windowless room in the rundown Hotel Iberia, which was managed by a cranky old man with apparently implacable nostalgia for a mythological Spanish past and unlimited scorn for the anti-coup resistance, whose alleged litany of violations of the norms of civilization he never ceased to recite. Things got especially bad when the Honduran coup regime decreed a 4 PM curfew and I became a one-woman captive audience to the Iberian's sermons on the latest transgressions of the delinquents, thugs, and hooligans who opposed the righteous "presidential succession" that had delivered Honduras from the grasp of the Zelaya-Chávez-Castro-Satan alliance. The only available palliative was a stockpile of the aptly named Imperial beer, which quickly ran out.

When the situation eventually became unsustainable, I relocated across town to a $5-per-night room in a hotel-restaurant complex run by a family that had immigrated from China some decades before, the patriarch of which was too consumed with business operations—including chasing

---

57 Rhodan, Maya. "Honduras Is Still the Murder Capital of The World." *Time Magazine*, 17 February 2014.

off drunks and other potential troublemakers with an ever-present base-ball bat—to inflict his political opinions on the clientele.

This hotel was conveniently located not far from the Brazilian embassy, where Zelaya would take up residence after smuggling himself back into Honduras in September 2009. Also close by was the U.S. embassy, where I attended an August meeting between a human rights delegation and embassy officials who had not adequately rehearsed the U.S. line on the Honduran governmental switcheroo of June 28.[58]

After Deputy Mission Chief Simon Henshaw had broken the ice by pro-claiming his conviction that Zelaya's overthrow "was a coup and that it was a military coup and that it was wrong," U.S. Ambassador to Honduras Hugo Llorens arrived on the scene to rectify matters by detecting a "clear-cut case of a coup" and then downgrading it to the status of a "whatev-er-you-call-it." Llorens went on to assert that the joint U.S.-Honduran military base at Soto Cano had been "shut down," ostensibly as pun-ishment for this "whatever-you-call-it," although he then backtracked and acknowledged that U.S. troops were indeed still there but weren't talking to their Honduran counterparts. The delegation questioned why the postcoup repression of protesters by what Henshaw had described as Honduras' "extremely uneducated troops and policemen" had not resulted in a suspension of "education" for Honduran soldiers enrolled at the U.S. Army School of the Americas (SOA)—which, founded in Panama in 1946 and then transferred to Fort Benning, Georgia, had traditionally been the go-to institution for Latin American dictators,

---

58   I reported this meeting for *Narco News* prior to a dramatic falling-out with the editor, to be dis-cussed later in this chapter: "U.S. Ambassador Hugo Llorens Discloses Secrets of the Honduran Coup; Chinese Viewing Prohibited," 15 August 2009. https://www.narconews.com/Issue59/arti-cle3767.html

torturers, and death squad leaders.[59] Llorens triumphantly countered that the SOA no longer existed, after which he was reminded that the school had simply been renamed the Western Hemisphere Institute for Security Cooperation (WHINSEC).

A couple of months after this meeting, I had a rare opportunity to interview one particular SOA alumnus by the name of Romeo Vásquez Velásquez, the Honduran general who had spearheaded the coup.[60] As Vásquez was fond of telling the Honduran media, prior to the events of June he had been on the verge of retirement to a quiet family life, but God had devised other plans for him. Perhaps in support of this claim, he appeared at a televised mass on Honduran Armed Forces Day clutching a crucifix.

---

59 Among the long list of illustrious SOA alumni is the late Salvadoran Lieutenant Colonel Domingo Monterrosa Barrios, commander of the U.S.-trained and U.S.-equipped Atlacatl battalion, which, as *Jacobin Magazine* puts it, "carried out one of the worst massacres in the history of the Americas" at El Mozote, El Salvador, during that country's civil war. More than 800 people were slaughtered over the course of two days in 1981, in a bloodbath that included such performances as a Salvadoran major who "walked over, scooped a little boy from a crowd of kids, flung him into the air, and speared him with a bayonet as he came back down" (Uetricht, Micah and Branko Marcetic. "Remember El Mozote." 12 December 2016. https://jacobinmag.com/2016/12/el-mozote-el-salvador-war-reagan-atlacatl-massacre). As with so many "civil wars" in the region and beyond, the U.S. played a starring role in this one. A 1998 dispatch in *The Atlantic* summarized the atrocity: "The success of U.S. policy in El Salvador—preventing a [left-wing] guerrilla victory—was based on 40,000 political murders" (Schwarz, Benjamin. "Dirty Hands." December 1998. https://www.theatlantic.com/magazine/archive/1998/12/dirty-hands/377364/). It is this sort of trivia that should be continuously juxtaposed against any and all peeps that the U.S. makes about other countries' violations of international human rights standards.

60 My write-up of the interview can be accessed on the *CounterPunch* website: "An Interview with Honduran Coup General Romeo Vásquez Velásquez," 25 November 2009. https://www.counterpunch.org/2009/11/25/an-interview-with-honduran-coup-general-romeo-v-aacute-squez-velaacute-squez/. I first tried pitching a version of the piece to *The Progressive* magazine but was told by the editor that "I wasn't sure how much was made up, and how much was real." For the record, nothing was made up.

My total lack of credentials notwithstanding, an acquaintance at a Honduran radio station pulled some strings and put me in contact with Vásquez's assistant, Colonel Wilfredo García Rodríguez, another SOA alumnus who spent several weeks hanging up on me before grudgingly granting me an appointment at military headquarters. When I turned up at the appointed time, García announced that he had assumed I would be "old and fat" and proceeded to entertain me for two hours with tales like the time he saw Jennifer López in person.

The diminutive Vásquez took over from there and ushered me into his spacious office, which boasted a variety of religious paraphernalia, a wine rack, and a book about Western Sahara—which, it turned out, was not being considered as an exile destination for Zelaya but was simply the site of a UN mission in which Honduran troops participated. We took a seat side by side and commenced to have a jovial chat about the political intricacies of Honduras, where, Vásquez warned, "there will always be people who want to attain power through ways other than the proper way of being elected"—although it was not clear that he had fully thought through the implications of this line of reasoning given that he himself had just perpetrated a coup.

Contending that Zelaya's proposed nonbinding public-opinion survey had been "part of an international project commanded by Hugo Chávez," Vásquez assured me that the Honduran military was composed of "very democratic soldiers" who were conveniently also god-fearing, because "religiously devoted armies are generally the ones that win." He denied reports that Honduran troops and policemen had been blasting music at all hours of the night outside the Brazilian embassy in order to further disrupt the sleeping patterns and sanity of Zelaya and companions housed therein: "We are soldiers but we are not people who want to hurt anybody."

The image of Honduran soldiers as armed cherubs was repudiated by Human Rights Watch's write-up of the situation in Honduras in 2009, which specified that, in addition to engaging in lethal violence, "security forces also repeatedly used wooden batons, metal tubes, and chains to beat protesters," while there were coincidentally "no reports of protesters carrying or using lethal weapons." Among other documented trends was a "surge in rape, beatings, extortion, and arbitrary detention of transgender persons in Honduras by law enforcement officials."[61]

As my encounter with Vásquez came to an end, the general affirmed that the problem in Honduras was that there was in fact "too much liberty," which meant that members of the anti-coup resistance were able to run around "doing things they shouldn't be doing," such as "insulting people, dirtying walls" with graffiti, and "setting buildings on fire." Once I had turned off my tape recorder, Vásquez turned to me with all of the sex appeal one might expect from a short, aging coupmonger and informed me that he wouldn't at all mind acquiring a second wife. In light of the current political ambience in Honduras, I determined that the most prudent course of action was to smile, nod, and promise to call him.

*　　*　　*

While the Honduran *golpistas* and right-wing media didn't much care when protesters were injured or killed, any reports of potential vandalism by the anti-coup crowd was cause for hysteria. Coup president Micheletti, predictably baptized the "first national hero of the twenty-first century" by the Honduran National Industrial Association, took it upon himself to condemn the application of graffiti to the "walls of private and state-owned establishments and the

---

61 "Honduras: Events of 2009." Human Rights Watch World Report, 2010. https://www.hrw.org/world-report/2010/country-chapters/honduras

walls of churches" as "a great sin." Imperial fast food chains and other corporate iconography—all-pervasive features of the Honduran landscape—were also near and dear to right-wing hearts.

In August, for example, one of the Tegucigalpa branches of Popeye's was set ablaze following a month and a half of brutal military and police repression of peaceful marches. The ensuing grief and rage on behalf of this fast food restaurant was almost sufficient, it seemed, to merit a national day of mourning. When I later made the mistake of suggesting to a Honduran university student with designer sunglasses and an SUV that the anti-coup resistance was perhaps actually nonviolent, she resurrected the brief demise of Popeye's and put an end to my blasphemy, throwing in for good measure some demographic analysis: 80 percent of Hondurans were thugs, 80 percent of Hondurans were by coincidence also poor—lest there remain any doubt that poverty itself was a crime—and it was these statistics that were to blame for Zelaya's overwhelming popularity. Never mind that overwhelming popular support automatically made Zelaya a representative of Honduran democracy and not, as the SUV-er contended, its enemy.

Which brings us to one of the golden rules of the right: when democracy fails to deliver, invalidate the *demos*. From the perspective of the pro-coup crowd—many of whom had learnt the joys of democratic freedom from fancy shopping trips to my own exclusive homeland—the real *pueblo hondureño* was whatever the élite minority said it was, regardless of whatever thoughts the ignorant and uncivilized masses might have on the matter.[62] Meanwhile, the excessive violence perpetrated by the U.S.-backed

---

62 The assumption that the *demos* is not capable of making choices in its own best interest is of course nothing new, nor is it unique to Honduras. Various Middle Eastern locales also come to mind, where it is has been argued that, for cultural reasons, people require rule by an iron fist or at least by enlightened monarchs—an arrangement that often works out well for the Western oil and defense industries, among other corporate stakeholders (for more examples of how the

Honduran state against a range of domestic have-nots was in no way whatsoever to blame for Honduras' increasingly violent state of affairs; ditto for the U.S. habit of inundating the region with weapons.

For some idea of what non-élite Hondurans have traditionally been up against, it's useful to revisit a 2002 report on Honduras from the United Nations Commission on Human Rights, in which Special Rapporteur Asma Jahangir warned that "every child with a tattoo and street child is stigmatized as a criminal who is creating an unfriendly climate for investment and tourism in the country." The popularity of this attitude coupled with "institutionalized impunity" had, Jahangir noted, resulted in a pattern of extrajudicial killing of children by Honduran security forces: "In most of the cases the child was unarmed and did not provoke the police to use force, let alone lethal force."[63]

Nor did the extrajudicial business subside in subsequent years. When I met in 2009 with María Luisa Borjas, the former chief of internal affairs for the Honduran police, she lamented that some 3,000 young persons had

---

anti-democratic nature of the Gulf states serves the objectives of the international capitalist system headed up by the U.S. and valiantly backed by the UK, see Wearing, David. *AngloArabia: Why Gulf Wealth Matters to Britain.* Cambridge: Polity Press, 2018). In Iran, the opposition's self-identification as the real Iranian people is fully endorsed by the U.S., which salivates at the prospect of a Western-oriented, materialistic Iranian nation spontaneously surging forth from the ruins of theocracy, whereupon it will cease to bitch about the transgressions of the Great and Little Satans and everyone will live happily ever after. In Venezuela under Hugo Chávez, meanwhile, rich Venezuelans pissed about having to share the country's wealth cast themselves as the real *pueblo*—a scheme that erased the millions of people under Chávez who were at last granted the chance of a dignified existence. The U.S. spilled many tears over the plight of the poor rich Venezuelans—even backing one of those oh-so-democratic coup attempts in 2002. Nor, it seems, does the U.S. trust its own citizens with democracy. Hence, the electoral college.

63 UN Commission on Human Rights. *Extrajudicial, summary or arbitrary executions: Report submitted pursuant to Commission on Human Rights resolution 2002/36: Addendum - Mission to Honduras,* 14 June 2002, E/CN.4/2003/3/Add.2, available at: http://www.refworld.org/docid/3dec85782.html

been murdered by the state during the presidency of Zelaya's predecessor Ricardo Maduro (2002–06). The killing spree had been made possible, Borjas said, by a de facto criminalization of youth and a liberal application of the term "gang member"—a policy inspired by none other than the "zero tolerance" approach of ex–New York mayor Rudy Giuliani.

American University anthropologist Dr. Adrienne Pine specifies in her book *Working Hard, Drinking Hard: On Violence and Survival in Honduras* that Maduro's war on crime—and the blanket blaming of all violence on gangs—"led to increasing gang militarization in a war of escalation, thus creating a real version of the monstrous creature that had formerly been largely a product of colonialist imagination."[64] In other imaginative sequences, Oscar Álvarez—Maduro's security minister, a living symbol of extrajudicial killing, and the nephew of late Battalion 316 commander and SOA attendee General Gustavo Álvarez Martínez—was recycled into the very same ministerial position under Porfirio Lobo, the winner of the illegitimate postcoup elections of November 2009. As of 2018, Álvarez's LinkedIn profile listed him as a Texas-based consultant "specializing in Latin American investment," with an impressive professional history of "work[ing] closely with United States agencies in the fight against organized crime, drug trafficking, terrorism, human trafficking, and gangs."

Pine observes that, in Honduras, "the language of war resonates with many poor people . . . who tend to forget that they themselves will be the victims of a war on crime" and will often be "labeled criminals by virtue of class and geography."[65] Case in point: my Honduran friend Mariano, whom I met in 2009 at the fruit and vegetable stand he operated on the

---

64 Pine, Adrienne. *Working Hard, Drinking Hard: On Violence and Survival in Honduras*. Berkeley and Los Angeles: University of California Press, 2008, p. 75.

65 *Ibid.*, p. 62.

corner of a busy Tegucigalpa street, endorsed iron fist policies by the state as a consequence of the obstacles to survival he had faced in Honduras, such as being shot at. Though Mariano acknowledged that government crime-fighting initiatives were generally also criminal in nature, he concluded that there was no other choice but the *mano dura*—despite the fact that there was nothing about his "class and geography" that saved him from future victimization.

I myself never fully experienced the hazards of existence in Honduras, free as I was to come and go as I pleased without having to worry about militarized borders and criminalized migration patterns. I did, however, get a taste of egregiously weaponized environments in which the ubiquity of armaments ostensibly intended for "security" appeared to produce exactly the opposite effect. Beyond the whole issue of preposterous force unleashed against protesters by Honduran military and police, it wasn't enormously reassuring to find coffee shops, gas stations, and nearly every other variety of establishment under the sun equipped with armed guards. In other words, while the older man with the decrepit shotgun stationed at my internet café of choice was as polite as could be and a swell conversationalist, I can safely say that my sense of personal security would have been significantly enhanced sans his presence.

Not that personal security was, as far as I could tell, ever really an option. Although I never went outside with much more than a black plastic bag containing a minimal amount of money and a crappy cell phone, I was accosted on several occasions and threatened with death unless I handed something over. One time, this meant parting with five dollars and an alarm clock, the latter item being ultimately restituted to me. Another time, my would-be assailant announced that he was armed with a gun, which I didn't think was necessarily the case but nevertheless suggested that we go in search of an ATM. In the end, the issue of my lack of any sort of ATM card was rendered irrelevant by my companion's decision that I was nice enough and could therefore adopt his 18-month-old son, who, he said, was improperly cared for on account of the child's mother's crack habit.

During an excursion to the northern coast of Honduras to speak with Afro-indigenous and other resistance groups, I awoke one night to find that an unknown man had inserted himself into my second-floor room after cutting away the window screen and removing the glass slats. A bout of demented screaming drove him back out the window as I dashed into the hall in my underwear, never to sleep again.

At the time, I was temporarily employed at the lamely branded *Narco News* operation overseen by Mexico-based U.S. citizen Al Giordano, who had promptly commenced dispatching emails threatening to "burst into a supernova" at the prospect of our impending union: "Do you think that if I came down to Honduras you might take me in your arms and begin a new level of relationship and collaboration?"

Come down to Honduras he did, where he was forcibly deflected from my arms and busied himself further disseminating his message of nonviolent resistance to the Honduran masses. Finding an audience with a smattering of anti-coup organizations, Giordano approached these lectures with an air of leftist camaraderie, telling and retelling the marvelous tale of the Serbian Revolution of 2000 that nonviolently overthrew Slobodan Milošević—in what was naturally a great victory for the neoliberal order, though that part was left out of the speech.

Also touching down briefly in postcoup Honduras was a giant sketchball by the name of Ivan Marović, self-declared Serbian revolutionary hero and, like Giordano, backed by the International Center on Nonviolent Conflict (ICNC), an outfit run by a grotesquely wealthy American investor and other concerned members of the global populace. As my foolish naivety lessened over time, I came to better comprehend the function of these imperial emissaries with faux subversive credentials—particularly when Marović later took it upon himself to detail, for the benefit of pupils at Giordano's so-called "Authentic Journalism School" in Mexico, his previous efforts to shove nonviolence down the throats of folks in occupied Palestine: "The Palestinians kept talking about how they are being wronged. I wish I could tell them how much THEY are wrong."[66]

To be sure, there's nothing about decades of Israeli ethnic cleansing and massacres of Palestinians that can't be rectified by a Palestinian decision to roll over and submit. My own stint with *Narco News* was mercifully cut short when Giordano got rid of me after:

1. determining that I was conspiring to distract his readership from the Honduran struggle by talking about Israel, and
2. proposing a remedy to the situation that involved me living with him in Mexico City, where he would cook for me and fix my head.

As of 2018, cursory internet research revealed that Giordano had been slammed with sexual harassment allegations and that Marović had relocated to Kenya, where he was the proprietor of an unused blog titled

---

66 Quoted in D'Almeida, Kanya. "A Revolution Is Like 'Good Sex': The Ivan Marovic Story Is Coming to a Street Theater Near You." *The Narco News Bulletin*, 19 May 2011. https://narconews.com/Issue67/article4418.html

"Retired Revolutionary" and a devoted Instagrammer of nature and wild-life photos.[67]

*   *   *

Unsurprisingly, most Hondurans did not require gringo envoys to dictate to them the proper forms of resistance. Rather, the resilience and humanity exhibited day after day by anti-coup protesters served as an example for all of dignity under fire.

I attended various marches in the company of a severely diabetic school-teacher and his daughter from Zelaya's hometown of Catacamas, who supplied me with red bandanas and other resistance wear. Among the songs and chants frequently heard was the Argentine "*Nos tienen miedo porque no tenemos miedo*"—"They're afraid of us because we're not afraid"—which seemed to apply to pretty much everyone present except me. The vibrant solidarity of the crowds, which somehow never abated even after hours under the sun and the ever-present danger of military and police assault, was all the more noteworthy given what these crowds represented: this was not just about the rejection of an illegal coup or a demonstration of undy-ing dedication to the figure of Zelaya, this was about defiance of an entire history of right-wing attempts to crush the aspirations of a people.

---

67 For Giordano, see Higgins, Eoin. "We Probed Sexual Misconduct Claims Against Journalist Al Giordano. Here's What We Found." *Huffington Post*, 3 May 2018. In addition to standard harass-ment and manipulation of young women, Giordano reportedly also had some more unique tricks up his sleeve: "When he got sick with gout and couldn't move from his bed, he told [aspiring journalist Isadora] Bonilla to take the jars he filled with urine and empty and wash them, she said." As for Marović, the last entry at the Retired Revolutionary blog (http://www.retiredrevo-lutionary.com/) is dated February 2012, but his Instagram account offers all sorts of treats, such as "Elephant": https://www.instagram.com/p/Bdb3sUHgFMI/; and "White rhinos crossing the road": https://www.instagram.com/p/Bdbz57AAkRe/

When Zelaya surreptitiously repatriated himself in September 2009 and holed up in the Brazilian embassy in Tegucigalpa with a number of his supporters—an event that prompted reports in the ever-meticulous Honduran media of men sleeping in the arms of other men on the embassy floor—the surrounding neighborhood became another super-militarized point of protest. I began regular trips to the embassy after an acquaintance of mine on the inside requested that I attempt to smuggle him some pens, a mission for which I appealed to a man named Alex Palencia, who as a volunteer with the Committee for the Defense of Human Rights in Honduras (CODEH) was tasked with overseeing the delivery of food and other necessary items to the embassy's long-term guests. The pens were swiftly confiscated by Honduran security forces, and Palencia suggested I try to find pens that didn't look like pens.

This, however, was easier said than done, as nearly everything, it seemed, qualified as potential dual-use material necessitating interception. At one point I had Palencia jot down a list for me of all of the items CODEH had been thwarted from delivering, which included pillows, apples, tennis shoes, batteries, vitamins, peanuts, pants, jackets, eggnog, shampoo, tinfoil, nail clippers, shoelaces, socks, gum, metal utensils, pastries, shaving cream, and the Bible, to name just a few. Why the Bible of all things was halted by a regime with such professed proximity to the Lord was never clear, but Palencia speculated it had something to do with the presence inside the embassy of a popular anti-coup Salvadoran priest and environmental activist named José Andrés Tamayo Cortez, with whom the Honduran powers that be did not care to share their monopoly over the word of God.

When not battling security forces over shoelaces and forks, Palencia was a musician and composer driven by a vision of an eventual rock opera about the life and work of Francisco Morazán, nineteenth-century Honduran hero, liberator, and "public enemy of political and religious mediocrity," as Palencia put it. The contemporary Honduran ruling class, he contended, saw Morazán not as a national idol but rather as a "threat to the democratic principles they claim to represent," in which arrangement "democracy" meant the "maintenance at all cost of a system of government skewed in favor of an exploitative minority, to the detriment of the majority." In other words: the U.S. model in a nutshell. And indeed, the recurrent U.S. role as public enemy in the literal sense—for publics both within and beyond its borders—was far from lost on the Honduran resistance.

Flash forward to 2012 and a *New York Times* op-ed titled "In Honduras, a Mess Made in the U.S.," which one can only assume made it onto the paper's pages thanks to some fluke involving a comatose or otherwise incapacitated editor. Detailing Honduras' postcoup descent "deeper into a human rights and security abyss" that was "in good part the State Department's making," University of California scholar Dana Frank slammed the administration of Barack Obama for recognizing the fraudulent November 2009 elections that brought Porfirio Lobo to power.

Citing reports that more than 300 people had thus far been killed by state security forces since the coup, with at least 34 members of the Honduran opposition disappeared or killed, Frank noted that no fewer than 13 journalists had furthermore been reported murdered since Lobo's ascension to office. And yet the U.S., true to form, had "maintained and in some areas increased military and police financing for Honduras [while] enlarging its military bases there."[68]

In a 2014 dispatch for *Al Jazeera America*, Mark Weisbrot of the Center for Economic and Policy Research in Washington, DC, highlighted some related aspects of the coup fallout for which Washington was more than

---

68 Frank, Dana. "In Honduras, a Mess Made in the U.S.." *New York Times*, 26 January 2012. https://www.nytimes.com/2012/01/27/opinion/in-honduras-a-mess-helped-by-the-us.html

slightly responsible: "The homicide rate in Honduras, already the highest in the world, increased by 50 percent from 2008 to 2011; political repression, the murder of opposition political candidates, peasant organizers and LGBT activists increased and continue to this day. Femicides skyrocketed."[69]

Of course, state repression in Honduras is more than compatible with U.S. financial interests and corporate exploitation. And what do you know: the slogan of the Lobo government was nothing other than "Honduras Is Open for Business." This was a relief to international investors fearful at the prospect of the country's economic sovereignty, but decidedly less heartening for Hondurans whose lives happened to stand in the way of "business." According to the NGO Global Witness, for example, Honduras was the "deadliest country in the world for environmental activism" in 2017.[70] Among those recently assassinated was Berta Cáceres, a fierce campaigner for indigenous land rights and against environmentally destructive megaprojects.

The Guardian's Nina Lakhani, relaying the claim by a former Honduran soldier that Cáceres' name had appeared on a hitlist belonging to U.S.-trained Honduran special forces, stressed that human rights groups had warned the U.S. Congress "that death squads were targeting opposition activists [in Honduras], much like they did during the 'dirty war' in the 1980s."[71] To put

69 Weisbrot, Mark. "Hard choices: Hillary Clinton admits role in Honduran coup aftermath." *Al Jazeera America*, 29 September 2014. http://america.aljazeera.com/opinions/2014/9/hillary-clinton-honduraslatinamericaforeignpolicy.html

70 "Honduras: The Deadliest Country in the World for Environmental Activism." *Global Witness*, 31 January 2017. https://www.globalwitness.org/ru/campaigns/environmental-activists/honduras-deadliest-country-world-environmental-activism/

71 Lakhani, Nina. "Berta Cáceres's name was on Honduran military hitlist, says former soldier." *The Guardian*, 21 June 2016. https://www.theguardian.com/world/2016/jun/21/berta-caceres-name-honduran-military-hitlist-former-soldier

it a different way: Honduras was not just open for business, it was back in business.

And in business it has remained under Juan Orlando Hernández, who was reelected in November 2017 in a vote widely denounced as extremely dubious (as previously mentioned, his reelection was made possible by scrapping the constitutional article limiting presidents to a single term—the very article that Zelaya was accused of violating and that was used as grounds for his overthrow). Post-election protests triggered a typically lethal response from the Honduran forces of law and order, while, in the midst of the vicious crackdown, the *New York Times* informed readers that the U.S. State Department had just "certified that Honduras was meeting human rights conditions, strengthening transparency, and cracking down on corruption"—a prerequisite for the release of yet more U.S. aid to those very same forces.[72]

Given the context of pervasive violence and insecurity, it's not difficult to surmise why loads of Hondurans might uproot themselves and flee northward to the U.S. at great personal risk, only to face criminalization by the logic of empire—which mandates that the majority of inferior imperial subjects remain confined to their appointed geographical spaces to consume U.S. products, ingest Popeyes and Taco Bell, and basically suck it up and deal with whatever obscene brutality might come their way. A certain influx of undocumented migrants is, however, required to keep key U.S. industries running, as well as to serve as a readymade national scapegoat and bogeyman justifying ever more neurotic border fortification plans.[73] In

---

72 Malkin, Elisabeth. "U.S. at a Crossroad as It Confronts Turmoil in Honduras." *New York Times*, 13 December 2017. https://www.nytimes.com/2017/12/13/world/americas/honduras-election-juan-orlando-hernandez.html

73 See Dudley, Mary Jo. "These U.S. industries can't work without illegal immigrants." CBS News, 25 June 2018. https://www.cbsnews.com/news/illegal-immigrants-us-economy-farm-workers-taxes/

the early summer of 2018, brutality on the U.S. frontier itself was producing headlines along the lines of: "Split from his family at border, Honduran asylum seeker hangs himself in Texas jail"—an event that, as the *Washington Post* wrote in June, took place "not long after the Trump administration began implementing its 'zero-tolerance' crackdown on illegal migration, measures that include separating parents from their children."[74]

Then along came the U.S.-bound migrant caravan, which, originating in the Honduran city of San Pedro Sula in October 2018, attracted thousands of Central Americans hoping to reach the U.S. by foot—a journey which would take well over a month. The decision to travel as a large group mitigated the dangers generally faced by migrants, including murder, disappearance, and rape. Predictably, the mass of peaceful pedestrians slowly inching their way northward lit a fire under Trump's ass, and he took to Twitter to warn that "criminals and unknown Middle Easterners are mixed in" with the caravan: "I have alerted Border Patrol and Military that this is a National Emergy [*sic*]."[75] Ten days later, he threatened to dispatch as many as 15,000 additional troops to the southern border—on top of all of the personnel already stationed there—to fend off the encroaching enemy.[76] After all, there is pretty much no better way to attack the U.S. than by walking there from Honduras.

---

74 See Brumfield, Loyd. *Dallas News*, 9 June 2018. https://www.dallasnews.com/news/texas/2018/06/09/honduran-man-upset-separated-family-hangs-south-texas-jail, and Miroff, Nick. "A family was separated at the border, and this distraught father took his own life." The *Washington Post*, 9 June 2018. https://www.washingtonpost.com/world/national-security/a-family-was-separated-at-the-border-and-this-distraught-father-took-his-own-life/2018/06/08/24e40b70-6b5d-11e8-9e38-24e693b38637_story.html

75 @realDonaldTrump, 22 October 2018. https://twitter.com/realdonaldtrump/status/1054351078328885248

76 "Trump says border troops could hit 15K, surprising Pentagon." Associated Press, 1 November 2018. https://www.cnbc.com/2018/11/01/trump-says-border-troops-could-hit-15k-surprising-pentagon.html

But while Trump & Co. battened down the hatches, a critical history lesson was lost in the ruckus: U.S. foreign policy in Central America over the past several decades is largely to blame for U.S.-bound migration in the first place. It's no coincidence that the caravan initiated in Honduras, the epicenter of recent U.S. meddling in the region. And yet the U.S. commitment to nurturing a violent Central American milieu is nothing new; back in 1954, for instance, the CIA-orchestrated coup against democratically elected Guatemalan president Jacobo Árbenz—a character insufficiently obsequious to U.S. corporate interests—paved the way for a war in which more than 200,000 Guatemalans were killed or disappeared, many of them indigenous Mayans. From Guatemala to El Salvador and Honduras and beyond, it's difficult to argue that U.S. support for dictators, death squads, and egregious socioeconomic inequality has nothing to do with the present panorama of poverty and violence that Central Americans are fleeing. If anyone's suffering from a National "Emergy," it's them.

The U.S. obsession with the sacrosanctity of its own borders clearly hasn't stopped it from violating everyone else's. But there's no time to waste contemplating double standards when evil incarnate is coming at you from all directions—hence the utility of converting a caravan of humans seeking a better life into a nebulous mass of criminal-terrorist-gang-member-rapists. Honduran president Hernández meanwhile did his own part to spice things up by proclaiming the whole shebang a leftist conspiracy financed by Venezuela.

It's like a scene out of the Cold War circa 1986, when that pre-Twitter Emergy known as Sandinista Nicaragua compelled President Reagan to address his fellow Americans on the matter of the "mounting danger in Central America that threatens the security of the United States." Nicaragua, a mere "two hours' flying time from our own borders," was at the time the go-to spot for international evildoers, harboring "Soviets, East Germans,

Bulgarians, North Koreans, Cubans and terrorists from the P.L.O. and the Red Brigades" and endorsed by "Arafat, Qaddafi, and the Ayatollah Khomeini," Furthermore, the president professed to "know [that] every American parent concerned about the drug problem will be outraged to learn that top Nicaraguan Government officials are deeply involved in drug trafficking"—though parents would presumably have been more outraged to learn that the U.S. and its Contra mercenaries were up to their ears in the drug business and more than slightly to blame for the crack cocaine epidemic that devastated South Central Los Angeles.[77]

The moral of the story, according to Reagan, was that there was no conceivable "greater tragedy than for us to sit back and permit this cancer to spread"—i.e. the U.S. needed to funnel more money to the "freedom fighters struggling to bring democracy to their country and eliminate this Communist menace at its source." This would also, incidentally, help to avert a situation in which "desperate Latin peoples by the millions would begin fleeing north into the cities of the southern United States, or to wherever some hope of freedom remained."[78] As for how the noble battle for freedom played out in reality, Noam Chomsky has described the U.S. Contra war as a "large-scale terrorist war against Nicaragua, combined with economic warfare that was even more lethal."[79]

Luckily for the U.S., there is no shortage of imperial lapdogs who claim that the gringos have brought only good things to Central America. Back in 2000, for example, Thomas Friedman crowed with delight over the perks of life in the Honduran homeland: "Honduras, little Honduras, already

---

77 See Cockburn, Alexander and Jeffrey St. Clair. *Whiteout: The CIA, Drugs and the Press.* New York: Verso, 1998.

78 "Transcript of the President's Speech." *New York Times,* 17 March 1986. https://www.nytimes .com/1986/03/17/world/transcript-of-the-president-s-speech.html

79 Chomsky, Noam. *What Uncle Sam Really Wants.* Berkeley: Odonian Press, 2002, p. 42.

exports seven times more textiles and apparel to the U.S. than all 48 nations of sub-Saharan Africa combined."[80] He followed up this absurdity five years later with an intervention on behalf of the Central American Free Trade Agreement (CAFTA), according to which, he explained, the U.S. would altruistically offer Central America the opportunity to engage in "labor-intensive sewing" and thereby "help consolidate these fragile democracies by locking in a trading relationship with the U.S. that is critical for their development." He subsequently boasted in reference to the article: "I wrote a column supporting the CAFTA, the Caribbean Free Trade initiative [sic]. I didn't even know what was in it. I just knew two words: free trade."[81]

With little Honduras now locked into an ever-tighter bond of economic servitude and human rights obliteration disguised as democracy consolidation, one can't help but feel that, in terms of empire-building, Honduras has been one hell of a coup indeed.

---

80 Friedman, Thomas. "Don't Punish Africa." *New York Times*, 7 March 2000. https://www.nytimes.com/2000/03/07/opinion/foreign-affairs-don-t-punish-africa.html

81 Quoted in Solomon, Norman. "Announcing the P.U.-litzer Prizes for 2006." *Fairness & Accuracy In Reporting*, 26 December 2006. https://fair.org/media-beat-column/announcing-the-p-u-litzer-prizes-for-2006/

Somewhere outside Addis Ababa, Ethiopia, 2016—or 2008, if you prefer the Ethiopian calendar.

Hitsats refugee camp for Eritrean refugees in northern Ethiopia, where Western NGOs have been known to deploy "humanitarianism" as a means of keeping refugees out of Europe.

Ananuri, post-Soviet republic of Georgia, taken during a brief pause in wine and Georgian dumpling overdose.

Naghsh-e Jahan Square, Esfahan, Iran: a popular terrorist hangout.

View from Bayterek monument in Astana, Kazakhstan, where you may place your hand in a gilded handprint of dictator Nursultan Nazarbayev.

Osh bazaar, Bishkek, Kyrgyzstan.

Akkar, Lebanon, two hours north of Beirut—or 25, depending on traffic.

Down the street from my parents' apartment in Barcelona, Catalonia, Spain.

Dikwella, south Sri Lanka: paradise on earth, until white people like me destroy it.

Dushanbe, Tajikistan, following a visit to a Soviet-era sanatorium in the Tajik mountains, where treatment options include having one's vagina sprayed with radioactive radon water.

Sidi Bou Said, Tunisia, much-celebrated "success story" of the Arab Spring.

Fresh milk in Kayaköy, Turkey, formerly the village of Karmylassos and a victim of the forcible population exchange between Turkey and Greece in the 1920s.

Fethiye, Turkey, where many of my worldly possessions have resided since 2004.

Entebbe, Uganda, site of that famous Israeli hostage-rescue raid in 1976 during the reign of Idi Amin, self-proclaimed "Lord of All the Beasts of the Earth and Fishes of the Sea."

Floating market in Can Tho, Vietnam, a country where as usual I was welcomed with extreme generosity despite my own country's atrocities.

4. TURKEY

At around 10 p.m. on June 28, 2016, a suicide attack killed dozens at Istanbul's Atatürk airport. At the time, I was in the southwestern Turkish coastal town of Fethiye, at a waterfront restaurant where I had been lured by a Turkish friend—we'll call him Murat—with the promise of shrimp in garlic sauce and some apolitical conversation. The latter stipulation was necessitated by the additional presence of Murat's old university buddy, whom we'll call Cengiz.

I had known Murat, a bartender-turned-accountant from Fethiye, since 2004, when he had graciously permitted Amelia and me to intermittently invade his home. Cengiz was a former intelligence operative now on a brief holiday from a temporary posting in the primarily Kurdish city of Diyarbakır in Turkey's southeast. I had been given no details about his job, aside from the fact that he was assisting in the age-old Turkish struggle against "terrorism."

Over dinner, our innocuous seaside discussion of the phenomenon of strapless adhesive flip-flops was interrupted when Cengiz received a phone call re: the airport attack. He immediately unleashed a barrage of curse words against the Kurds, those harborers of a perennial bloodlust and determination to rip Turkey apart.

The meltdown lasted a few minutes, after which Cengiz took a breath and reasoned that, actually, this couldn't possibly be Kurdish handiwork; the perpetrators must have belonged to ISIS. I made the mistake of suggesting that perhaps his anti-Kurdish rant hadn't been merited and was promptly accused of terrorist sympathies, while Cengiz proceeded to unfurl other nationalist talking points such as that the problem in Turkey was not that the Kurds had too few rights but rather too many.

It's anyone's guess, of course, how a surplus of rights might apply to a population that has been repeatedly displaced and killed while also having its language criminalized along with an array of other aspirations to earthly dignity. In 2012, for example, Turkey's English-language newspaper *Today's Zaman*—now conveniently outlawed—noted that "members of the Doğubeyazıt Municipal Council in the [Turkish] province of Ağrı were given jail sentences of one month and 20 days, and the district mayor six months, for naming a park in the district after Kurdish poet and philosopher Ehmedê Xanî."[82]

More recently, a long-lasting state of emergency that was imposed following the thwarted July 2016 coup attempt against Turkish president and aspiring Leader for Life Recep Tayyip Erdoğan has enabled a massive crackdown on perceived enemies of the government—whether or not these "enemies" had anything to do with the would-be coup. Hence the ongoing proliferation not only of mind-blowing statistics on the rampant detention of academics, human rights workers, pro-Kurdish politicians, and other problematic characters, but also of reports of torture and other mistreatment by Turkish security forces of persons allegedly affiliated with the Kurdistan Workers' Party (PKK) and similarly undesirable outfits.[83]

---

82 Quoted in Fernández, Belén. "Insulting the Turkish nation." *Al Jazeera*, 4 June 2013. https://www.aljazeera.com/indepth/opinion/2013/06/20136415145190720.html

83 See "Turkey: Government crackdown suffocating civil society through deliberate climate of fear." Amnesty International, 26 April 2018. https://www.amnesty.org/en/latest/news/2018/04/

The state of emergency furthermore facilitated the detection of even more perilous threats to national security than Kurdish philosopher-poets, with Reuters observing in September 2016 that among the Turkish television channels shuttered for disseminating "terrorist propaganda" were Govend TV, "which plays folk music, and Zarok TV, which airs Kurdish-language children's cartoons."[84]

After my altercation with Cengiz, I was theatrically disowned by Murat but was later forgiven—a fortuitous turn of events seeing as a sizable percentage of my worldly possessions resided in his closet in Fethiye. Murat's own personal history of interaction with the Kurdish question included having performed a portion of his compulsory military service along the Turkish border with Iraq, where in the course of ostensibly combating mountain-based PKK guerrillas he sustained a severe wound to the arm. The injury had not, however, been PKK-induced, but had instead been the fault of his tank-mates, who, he said, had managed to explode some munition inside rather than outside the tank.

Though acknowledging that Kurdish civilians had indeed suffered as a result of Turkish military excesses, Murat was of the conviction that these were simply Things of the Past That the Kurds Needed to Get Over. Never mind that, in Turkey as everywhere, the past was ever present—or that I

turkey-government-crackdown-suffocating-civil-society-through-deliberate-climate-of-fear/; Morris, Chris. "Reality Check: The numbers behind the crackdown in Turkey." *BBC News*, 18 June 2018. https://www.bbc.com/news/world-middle-east-44519112; and "Turkey: Renewed Torture in Police Custody, Abductions." Human Rights Watch, 12 October 2017. https://www.hrw.org/news/2017/10/12/turkey-renewed-torture-police-custody-abductions

84 Yackley, Ayla Jean. "Turkey pulls plug on 20 radio, TV channels in postcoup emergency decree." *Reuters*, 30 September 2016. https://www.reuters.com/article/us-turkey-media-idUSKCN12012K

could hardly count the number of Turks I'd heard complain about being stabbed in the back by the Arabs in World War I.

*   *   *

Amelia and I arrived to Turkey in the spring of 2004 at the invitation of a Turkish man I had met on a previous visit to the country, who had proposed by email that the three of us rent an apartment together in Fethiye and work as entertainers at a local resort. While this had initially sounded like as good a plan as any for two people with no plans, it serendipitously fell through, and, having preemptively retired from the entertainment industry and extricated ourselves from the man's presence, Amelia and I were left to pursue hitchhiking and other projects.

At the time, Murat was just a new acquaintance, but he offered his house as a part-time base, as did a Kurdish fellow called Doğan who hailed from the southeastern Turkish city of Gaziantep and worked seasonally at a döner kebab establishment in Fethiye. Though Amelia and I rarely saw him on account of his schedule, Doğan found plenty of opportunities to load us up with gifts shipped by bus from Gaziantep for us and our mothers, whom he'd never met but who were nonetheless deemed worthy of scarves, tea sets, and assorted knick-knacks. Though my Turkish was practically nonexistent at the time and Doğan's command of English was limited to kebab-related vocabulary, he did manage to communicate his dream to one day open Elvis Presley Döner Kebab in Germany. As I lost track of Doğan after my first few stints in Fethiye, it's anyone's guess as to whether the Germans were ultimately so blessed.

Named for a martyred Ottoman aviator-hero, Fethiye is situated around a bay surrounded by hills and mountains, some of them featuring ancient Lycian tombs hewn into the cliff face. Like many Turkish locales, the town is awash in red and white Turkish flags that further multiply in accordance with national holidays, the onset of military service by area youth, the martyrdom of Turkish soldiers by "terrorists," and any other occasion requiring a surge in patriotism. The hill opposite Murat's balcony is branded with the slogan *"ŞEHİTLER ÖLMEZ VATAN BÖLÜNMEZ"*—meaning martyrs never die and the homeland will never be divided—a friendly reminder that it is still imperative to funnel the entire domestic male population into the armed forces, and conducive to chanting at marches given its catchy rhyme.

Another key decorative theme centers around the figure of Mustafa Kemal Atatürk, founder of the modern secular Republic of Turkey in 1923 following the demise of the Ottoman Empire, who appears in statues, portraits, and all manner of other tributes, his signature emblazoned onto the rear windshields of vehicles and tattooed onto forearms. In more recent years, the cult of Atatürk has faced increasingly stiff competition from the pious Erdoğan, who hasn't exactly been subtle in his efforts to become the number-one Turkish icon.

Just over the hill from Fethiye is Kayaköy, formerly the village of Karmylassos, which hosts the crumbling houses and other remains of the Greek Orthodox community that was forcibly removed in the 1920s as part of the so-called population exchange of Christians and Muslims between Turkey and Greece, courtesy of the Lausanne Treaty. The mass, traumatic uprooting of people, based solely on religious criteria, served the postwar drive for religious homogeneity but did not take into account cultural and linguistic orientation—many deported "Greeks," for example, spoke only Turkish, and vice versa—or the psychological fallout that tends to ensue when humans are torn from their homes. A 2018 *Al Jazeera* documentary on the exchange illustrates the transgenerational effects of loss, with an elderly Turkish second-generation exchangee from Greece choking back tears in front of the camera as he recounts how, on her deathbed, his grandmother had implored: "Take me to my homeland, my son, so I don't die here."[85]

Over at the *London Review of Books*, the British historian Perry Anderson observes that the Kurds, who "made up perhaps a quarter of the population" in the "ethnically cleansed Anatolia" of the 1920s, generally spoke little Turkish but were not eligible for expulsion given their subscription to Islam. Having supplied "shock troops" for the Armenian genocide and fought in Turkey's War of Independence, the Kurds had been promised by Atatürk "respect for their identity, and autonomy in the regions where they predominated"—a promise quickly broken when "Kurdish areas were stocked with Turkish officials, Kurdish place names were changed, and the Kurdish language banned from courts and schools."

A Kurdish revolt in 1925 led to "deportations, executions and systematic Turkification" of the country's southeast, while a nationwide Law for the Maintenance of Order "closed down opposition parties and press for the rest of the decade." And so it was that, on the heels of the Ottoman Turkish extermination of an estimated 1.5 million Armenians, a subtler form of genocide was perpetrated in tandem with the solidification of the new Turkish republic. "Officially," writes Anderson, "the Kurds had by now ceased to exist," having been instead "forcibly classified as Turks."[86]

Flash forward nearly a century, and the Kurds of Turkey still have not been permitted to define their own existence. I once had a top police official in Fethiye assert to me pointblank that most Kurds are terrorists—reassuring

---

85 *The Great Population Exchange.* Directed by Işıl Öçal. Posted at *Al Jazeera* website, 28 February 2018. https://www.aljazeera.com/programmes/aljazeeraworld/2018/02/great-population-exchange-turkey-greece-180220111122516.html

86 Anderson, Perry. "Kemalism." *London Review of Books*, 11 September 2008. https://www.lrb.co.uk/v30/n17/perry-anderson/kemalism

news, no doubt, from a Maintainer of Order in a country that is 20 percent Kurdish. On another occasion, I witnessed someone call the cops on a couple of boys listening to Kurdish music in their car. As in the United States, institutionalized prejudice dies hard.[87]

In southeast Turkey, meanwhile, recent years have seen renewed repression, house demolitions, forced displacement, and curfews—and by curfew I mean the kind where you're not allowed outside.[88] One epicenter of anguish is mainly Kurdish Diyarbakır—the aforementioned Cengiz's place of temporary employment—about which conflict *The Guardian* provided some context in an April 2016 dispatch: "In one of several attempts at self-rule in cities and towns across the region, activists announced local administrative autonomy for [the Diyarbakır district of] Sur in August last year. The government in Ankara responded with a violent crackdown." The title of the article was not surprising: "In a devastated Turkish town, teenagers dream of joining the Kurdish guerrillas."[89]

*   *   *

---

87 For an example of vehicle-related ethno-musical infractions in the U.S., see the 2012 murder in Florida of black teenager Jordan Davis by white person Michael Dunn. Davis' mother Lucy McBath writes at *Newsweek*: "Jordan was 17 when he was shot and killed while sitting in a car at a Jacksonville gas station, for the apparently 'threatening' behavior of listening to loud music with his friends. Jordan was unarmed, but he was a young black man. Now my beloved only son is gone." ("Don't use my son's death to expand Stand Your Ground," 9 April 2017. https://www .newsweek.com/jordan-davis-death-expand-stand-your-ground-florida-580927)

88 See Yıldız, Duygu. "Turkey's Sur district: Disobedience and Collective Punishment." *The Region*, 28 November 2017. https://theregion.org/article/12057-turkey-s-sur-district-disobedi-ence-and-collective-punishment, and "Turkish authorities impose 176 new curfews on villages, towns in Diyarbakır." *Hürriyet Daily News*, 14 February 2018. http://www.hurriyetdailynews .com/turkish-authorities-impose-176-new-curfews-on-villages-towns-in-diyarbakir-127318

89 Letsch, Constanze. *The Guardian*, 3 April 2016. https://www.theguardian.com/world/2016/ apr/03/diyarbakir-kurdish-teenagers-dream-of-becoming-guerrillas

Amelia and I had visited Diyarbakır once, in 2005, as part of a hitchhiking tour of Turkey and Syria. Arriving fatigued, we had shamefully taken advantage of the high police presence to convince certain members of said police to place us on a bus north to the Black Sea city of Trabzon—our next destination—for free. This was done with the help of some or other fabricated sob story, and enabled us to sleep for 500-plus kilometers. Perhaps as karmic punishment, we were then picked up hitchhiking by a seemingly reserved Turkish doctor who invited us for a barbecue in a remote area, consumed a bottle of alcohol, punched his fist through a windowpane, and commenced to chase us around, leaving us no choice but to hide dramatically beside a stream—facedown—until the coast was clear.

Minor mishaps aside, I have in my years of drifting through the Turkish Republic often enjoyed greater freedoms than some of the state's Kurdish citizens—such as, you know, the right to leave the house. And as it turns out, the very homeland from which I disentangled myself of my own free will has played no small role in precluding the attainment of a Kurdish homeland, not to mention more basic goals. At the same time, and in keeping with established tradition, the U.S. has been complicit in the uprooting of masses of people who, unlike me, haven't asked to be uprooted.

In his book *The New Military Humanism*, Noam Chomsky observes that the year 1994 "marked two records in Turkey, veteran *Washington Post* correspondent Jonathan Randal reported from the scene: it was 'the year of the worst repression in the Kurdish provinces,' and the year when Turkey became 'the biggest single importer of American military hardware and thus the world's largest arms purchaser.'"[90]

---

90 Chomsky, Noam. *The New Military Humanism: Lessons from Kosovo.* London: Pluto Press, 1999, p. 54.

A 1995 *Human Rights Watch* report confirmed that the Clinton administration "says it supplies Turkey with 80 percent of its foreign military hardware"—an arrangement blissfully unaffected by the State Department's own admission "that Turkey engages in gross abuses such as torture, extrajudicial executions and forced village evacuations" with the help of "U.S.-origin equipment, which accounts for most major items of the Turkish military inventory." Citing interviews with U.S. military personnel, HRW remarked that "it appears that Pentagon representatives in Ankara are more eager than ever to sell Turkey U.S. weapons, including M-60 tanks, helicopter gunships, cluster bombs, ground-to-ground missiles and small arms." The numerous "gross abuses" documented by HRW included reports of female guerrilla suspects being forcibly stripped naked, sexually violated, and then shoved out of helicopters by Turkish soldiers.

Between 1984 and 1995, HRW emphasized, Turkey's war with the PKK was estimated to have entailed "over 19,000 deaths, including some 2,000 death-squad killings of suspected PKK sympathizers, two million internally displaced, and more than 2,200 villages destroyed, most of which were burned down by Turkish security forces." In 1994, things were apparently so bad that Azimet Köylüoğlu, the Turkish State Minister for Human Rights, "declared that the security forces had engaged in 'state terrorism' by burning villages and forcibly evacuating villagers"—a statement he was "later forced to retract."[91] After all, there was only room for one terrorist in the national imagination.

Nowadays, America's counterterror alibi isn't the only one that's flimsy as ever. There was that time the Turkish air force accidentally eliminated 35 Kurdish civilians in northern Iraq, or the time Turkey got super-involved

---

91 "Weapons Transfers and Violations of the Laws of War in Turkey." Human Rights Watch, 1995. https://www.hrw.org/legacy/reports/1995/Turkey.htm

in that massively terroristic business known as the Syrian civil war.[92] Fortunately for the current Turkish government, there are now lots of parties onto whom the terrorist label can be deflected; in April 2018, for example, 14 staff members of Turkey's *Cumhuriyet* newspaper were sentenced to prison on terrorism charges.[93] As *The Guardian* had explained the previous year, *Cumhuriyet* had irked the ruling party in various ways, including by "embarrass[ing] the national intelligence service by revealing that it had transported weapons to rebels in Syria under the guise of humanitarian aid in 2014."[94]

The 2016 coup attempt, which the government attributed to the popular U.S.-based Turkish preacher and former Erdoğan ally Fethullah Gülen, has additionally rendered a sizable percentage of the Turkish population eligible for terrorism-related guilt and membership in the Fethullah Terrorist Organization (FETÖ)—a term the actual followers of Gülen naturally do not employ, but, hey, it's not their job to name things. The threshold for terrorist-hood is pretty low, and can consist of having an account at a certain bank.[95]

---

92 Aydınlı, Pınar. "Turkey acknowledges killing civilians in Iraq strike." *Reuters*, 29 December 2011. https://www.reuters.com/article/us-turkey-iraq-airstrike/turkey-acknowledges-killing-civilians-in-iraq-strike-idUSTRE7BS07C20111229. For a sample of Turkish contributions to the Syrian civil war, see Cockburn, Patrick. *The Jihadis Return: ISIS and the New Sunni Uprising*, in which he explained that Turkey "allows weapons and jihadist volunteers, many of them potential suicide bombers, to cross its 510-mile-long border into Syria" (New York: OR Books, 2014).

93 "Turkey: Journalists Convicted for Doing Their Jobs." Human Rights Watch, 27 April 2018. https://www.hrw.org/news/2018/04/27/turkey-journalists-convicted-doing-their-jobs

94 Shaheen, Kareem and Gözde Hatunoğlu. "Turkish journalist defends press freedom as grand trial begins." *The Guardian*, 24 July 2017. https://www.theguardian.com/world/2017/jul/24/turkish-journalist-defends-press-freedom-as-large-scale-trial-starts

95 See Atar, Ersan. "Depositing money in Bank Asya on Gülen's order proof of FETÖ membership" [in which, we learn in paragraph one, "on Gülen's order" simply means "after early 2014"]. *Daily Sabah*, 11 February 2018. https://www.dailysabah.com/investigations/2018/02/12/depositing-money-in-bank-asya-on-gulens-order-proof-of-feto-membership-1518386092. Bank Asya,

In December 2017, meanwhile, trials began for nearly 150 academics who signed a petition calling for a peaceful settlement to the conflict between the Turkish state and the PKK in Turkey's southeast—a clear case of dissemination of terrorist propaganda.[96] Incidentally, with the whole peace-is-terror inversion, Turkey seems to be borrowing a page from the Israeli playbook, according to which even sleep can be a violent terrorist activity.

Though Erdoğan has long sought to paint himself as preeminent hero of the Palestinians and a tough-guy critic of Israel—announcing to former Israeli president Shimon Peres that "when it comes to killing, you know well how to kill" and accusing the Jewish state of "inhumane state terrorism," both accurate assessments—the head of a racist state that uproots, tortures, and kills is probably not the most qualified verbal warrior against another racist state that uproots, tortures, and kills (albeit on a much grander scale).[97]

---

formerly one of Turkey's top banks, was founded by Gülenists—long before being a Gülenist was a crime. In a 2017 *New York Times Magazine* piece, Suzy Hansen recounted some scenes from the Turkish "terrorist" roundup—like when a doctor in Istanbul opened his door at 6 a.m. to find police officers waiting to inform him that, not only was he accused of trying to kill Erdoğan, he was also wanted "for attempting to destroy Turkey and for being a member of a terrorist organization." As it turned out, the only evidence of the doctor's malevolent plot was that, when he had returned to Turkey with his family after living abroad for several years, he'd opened an account at the closest bank to his house: Bank Asya. Hansen also supplied a rundown of some of the other casualties of the postcoup-attempt purge to date: "Fifteen universities, 1,000 schools, 28 TV channels, 66 newspapers, 19 magazines, 36 radio stations, 26 publishing houses and five news agencies have been shut down." ("Inside Turkey's Purge," 13 April 2017. https://www.nytimes .com/2017/04/13/magazine/inside-turkeys-purge.html)

96 See Butler, Judith and Başak Ertür. "In Turkey, academics asking for peace are accused of terrorism." *The Guardian*, 11 December 2017. https://www.theguardian.com/commentisfree/2017/ dec/11/erdogan-turkey-academics-terrorism-violence-kurdish-people, and "Turkey: Academics on Trial for Signing Petition." Human Rights Watch, 5 December 2017. https://www.hrw.org/ news/2017/12/05/turkey-academics-trial-signing-petition

97 Bennhold, Katrin. "Leaders of Turkey and Israel Clash at Davos Panel." *New York Times*, 29 January 2009. http://www.nytimes.com/2009/01/30/world/europe/30clash.html?_r=0; "Aid ship raid is Israeli state terrorism – Turkish PM." *Reuters*, 31 May 2010. https://www.reuters.com/

This is especially true when racist state #1 is simultaneously purchasing weapons from racist state #2.[98]

Writing in the late 1990s at the *Boston Review*, John Tirman, now the Executive Director of the Center for International Studies at MIT, discussed the "genocide committed against Turkey's Kurdish population, an intentional extermination of 'Kurdishness' that began in the first years of the Republic"—a description that inevitably calls to mind Israel's attempted eradication of Palestinian-ness.[99] Erdoğan's own accusation re: Israeli state terrorism was occasioned by the May 2010 IDF massacre of eight Turkish activists and one 19-year-old Turkish-American on board the *Mavi Marmara*, the flagship of a flotilla endeavoring to deliver aid to the besieged Gaza Strip, focal point of Israel's ongoing genocidal quest to wipe out Palestinian identity.

The Israeli government conducted its usual assault on logic, explaining that the seafaring humanitarian activists were in fact violent extremists with "ties to global Jihad" and that the Israeli commandos who had descended from helicopters onto the ship to shoot people were the real victims of the whole affair.[100] The Israeli Foreign Ministry dutifully created a Flickr album titled "Weapons found on *Mavi Marmara*" and uploaded a barrage of images involving marbles, kitchen knives, keffiyehs, a metal pail, and a slingshot

---

article/palestinians-israel-turkey-erdogan/aid-ship-raid-is-israeli-state-terrorism-turkish-pm-idUSLDE64U1UF20100531

98 See, for example, "Turkey sees no impact on Israel drone delivery." *Reuters*, 1 June 2010. https://www.reuters.com/article/israel-flotilla-turkey-defence/turkey-sees-no-impact-on-israel-drone-delivery-idUSANK00286820100601. Just because the Israelis attack your flotilla doesn't mean you shouldn't buy drones from them.

99 Tirman, John. "Atatürk's Children." *Boston Review*, December 1997/January 1998. http://bostonreview.net/archives/BR22.6/Tirman.html

100 See Black, Ian and Haroon Siddique. "Q&A: The Gaza Freedom flotilla." *The Guardian*, 31 May 2010. https://www.theguardian.com/world/2010/may/31/q-a-gaza-freedom-flotilla

decorated with pink and purple stars featuring the green handwritten label "HIZBULLAH."[101] It was never explained whether the Lebanese militant group always labels its Gaza-bound slingshots in English, or why the photograph was initially specified as having been taken on February 7, 2006, i.e. more than four years prior to the seaborne global Jihadist plot.

I attended the funeral ceremony at Istanbul's Beyazıt mosque for Cevdet Kılıçlar, one of the murdered activists, an event that drew thousands of men, women, and children despite the June heat. A multitude of Palestinian flags joined the Turkish ones, and I procured souvenirs in the form of green headbands reading *"HEPİMİZ FİLİSTİNLİYİZ"*—"We are all Palestinians." I also procured bananas from a man with a wooden cart outside the mosque, where I spoke to another banana customer who confessed to having previously sympathized with Israel over its "terror" problem. That sympathy ended, he said, when he sat down and calculated the ratio of Israeli civilian deaths to Palestinian ones.

Thomas Friedman, for his part, assigned quotation marks to the flotilla's "humanitarian" activists—much as he had done with the Afghan "civilians" who were supposedly "casualties" of U.S. airstrikes—and turned up two weeks later at Istanbul's Özyeğin University to deliver one of his heavily compensated speeches.[102] In it, he covered important topics such as how

---

101 The Flickr album can be viewed here: https://www.flickr.com/photos/israel-mfa/4666095852/in/album-72157624179998488/; the closeup of the slingshot is here: https://www.flickr.com/photos/israel-mfa/4666095852/in/album-72157624179998488/, complete with caption encouraging viewers to "Note name engraved on handle."

102 Friedman, Thomas. "When Friends Fall Out." *New York Times*, 1 June 2010. https://www.nytimes.com/2010/06/02/opinion/02friedman.html; "Terrorist Software." *New York Times*, 23 November 2001. https://www.nytimes.com/2001/11/23/opinion/foreign-affairs-terrorist-software.html (in which we learn that, despite "all the nonsense written in the press—particularly the European and Arab media—about the concern for 'civilian casualties' in Afghanistan," in fact "many of those Afghan 'civilians' were praying for another dose of B-52's to liberate them

"a lot of bad stuff happens in the world without America, but not a lot of good stuff," which might have been news to Kılıçlar and the other "casualties" of the United States' favorite army.[103]

I found myself in Istanbul again in June 2013, when I was meant to be visiting Murat in Fethiye but apparently couldn't pass up the chance to be tear-gassed. This was during the Gezi Park protests, when unarmed demonstrators opposed to the destruction of one of the city center's last green spaces—and more generally to the authoritarian imposition of neoliberal "development" schemes—were assailed repeatedly by Turkish riot police, resulting in a number of deaths and more than 8,000 injuries as of early July, according to Amnesty International's report, "Gezi Park Protests: Brutal Denial of the Right to Peaceful Assembly in Turkey."

The report includes other highlights of the strife, such as *CNN Türk*'s infamous decision "to air a pre-scheduled two-hour documentary on penguins during the first weekend of mass protest across Turkey" and Erdoğan's suggestion "that banging pots and pans in solidarity with the demonstrators . . . would also be considered a crime."[104]

My introduction to tear gas took place one fine day when, after spending time at Gezi Park, an American friend and I relocated to a nearby bar off of Istanbul's iconic İstiklal Street. The park had been filled with tranquil

---

from the Taliban, casualties or not"). For an idea of the obscene speaking fees Friedman accrues, consider that, back in 2009, his fee per speech was $75,000, i.e. more money than I have earned cumulatively in the past decade (Rainey, James. "Thomas L. Friedman and the high cost of speaking." *Los Angeles Times*, 13 May 2009. http://articles.latimes.com/2009/may/13/entertainment/et-onthemedia13).

103   Quoted in Fernández, Belén. *The Imperial Messenger: Thomas Friedman at Work*. New York: Verso, 2011, p. 2.

104   "Gezi Park Protests: Brutal Denial of the Right to Peaceful Assembly in Turkey." Amnesty International, October 2013. https://www.amnestyusa.org/files/eur440222013en.pdf

people sharing food, conversation, books, and music—a far cry from the picture Erdoğan had painted of foreign terrorist infiltrators and alcoholic hooligan bandit-looters. My friend and I barely had time to start on our beers when the orders were given to attack the park, causing protesters to flee down İstiklal and surrounding arteries. Tear gas canisters were fired down our street, engulfing the bar with smoke. As any moderately resilient person would do, I dug my nails into the stranger nearest to me and begged him not to let me die—though he would certainly have been forgiven for ignoring my plea, given that all manner of attractive mucous had begun abundantly flowing from my nose and mouth as I writhed around in preparation for impending asphyxiation. In the end, death was staved off with the help of some protesters who had taken refuge in the bar and who doused me with antacid solution. An extraordinary amount of beer took care of the rest.

*   *   *

When in July 2016 another calamity registered on the contemporary Turkish timeline, I had just left Murat's place in Fethiye for the south of Italy. I watched the coverage of the attempted coup d'état on Italian television with my friend's mother, a sexagenarian from a small village in Puglia who asked what a *colpo di stato* was and whether or not it was democratic. I said no and she nodded: "I understand, it's communism."

If only.

As Erdoğan proceeded to exploit the coup to kill every possible bird with one stone, I was concerned that Murat might get caught up in the mess since, several years before, he had been roped by some acquaintances into attending Gülenist meetings in Fethiye. In fact, when Murat met up with me in Argentina in 2008, we paid a visit to a Gülen school in Buenos Aires, where we were treated to lunch and I was kindly given an anti-suicide bombing book in Spanish. Murat was ultimately left untouched by the postcoup witch-hunt, but one acquaintance of his was thrown in jail and another deemed it prudent to flee the country.

Now, the boundaries of permissible discourse in Turkey remain as restricted as ever. In comments made to me in 2017, Eyüp Burç—general coordinator of IMC TV, a pro-Kurdish station forced off the air the previous year with the help of the ever-handy "terrorist propaganda" charge—brought up the issue of Article 301 of the Turkish penal code, an intriguing feature of Turkish justice that formerly criminalized insults to "Turkishness" and has since been amended to criminalize insults to "the Turkish nation" and government institutions.[105]

As Burç saw it, freedom of the press and freedom of expression had already been definitively eradicated—a free press having "always been regarded by the state as an enemy, since it was and still is the only tool able to confront the state with the truth on issues like the Kurdish question." Next on the list, he contended, was freedom of thought.

Of course, leaders of the Turkish nation have long considered a monopoly on thought crucial to success. Just as the powers that be in the U.S. have

---

105 For IMC TV, see Uras, Umut. "Turkey shuts down TV channel over 'terror propaganda.'" *Al Jazeera*, 5 October 2016. https://www.aljazeera.com/news/2016/10/turkey-shuts-tv-channel-terror-propaganda-161004173625008.html. For an example of scenarios that have merited the application of Article 301, recall the 2005 trial of internationally renowned Turkish writer Orhan Pamuk. As English PEN put it in a letter to the editors at *The New York Review of Books*: "The charges stem from an interview given by Orhan Pamuk to the Swiss newspaper *Tages Anzeiger* on February 6, 2005, in which he is quoted as saying that 'thirty thousand Kurds and a million Armenians were killed in these lands and nobody but me dares to talk about it'" ("The Case of Orhan Pamuk," 15 December 2005. https://www.nybooks.com/articles/2005/12/15/the-case-of-orhan-pamuk/).

found it fruitful to inculcate the American public with cheery fairy-tale myths involving Pilgrims, Indians, and cranberry sauce to distract from the fact that the country happens to be founded on genocide and slavery, Turkey has generated its own myths to guard against challenges to legitimacy.

In his *London Review of Books* essay, Anderson writes of the "most extravagant mythology" fashioned under Atatürk: "By the mid-1930s, the state was propagating an ideology in which the Turks . . . had spread civilization from Central Asia to the world, from China to Brazil; and as the drivers of universal history, spoke a language that was the origin of all other tongues, which were derived from the Sun-Language of the first Turks."

According to Anderson, this sort of "ethnic megalomania reflected the extent of the underlying insecurity and artificiality of the official enterprise."[106] And while Erdoğan may not be so keen about propagating the myths of Atatürk, the zealous exertion of control over physical and ideological spaces has proved an enduring method of compensation for insecurity. In December 2017, *Middle East Eye* reported that the city of Istanbul had undertaken to rename nearly 200 streets containing the word *Gülen* or any other potential reminders of Erdoğan's erstwhile ally.

Additionally slated for rebranding were *Kandil* (oil lamp) Street—since "this is also the name of the group of mountains in northern Iraq where the [PKK] has its base"—as well as "morally inappropriate" thoroughfares like *Aşkım* (my love) Street. "By comparison," *Middle East Eye* noted, an Istanbul municipality run by Erdoğan's party had "caused controversy in

---

106 Anderson, Perry. "Kemalism." *London Review of Books*, 11 September 2008. https://www.lrb .co.uk/v30/n17/perry-anderson/kemalism

July after it changed the name of a road to that of one of the founders of al-Qaeda."[107]

Likewise in December 2017, I had the opportunity to observe postcoup Turkish landscape and infrastructure renovations firsthand when I devised a brilliant scheme involving a 24-hour bus ride from the Georgian city of Kutaisi to Istanbul and a giant vat of Georgian wine I had purchased for my parents, which rode in my lap. As the arrangement precluded sleep, I spent the time counting all the bridges, overpasses, and forests along Turkey's northern coast that had been renamed in honor of the new coup martyrs.

In Turkey's primarily Kurdish southeast, on the other hand, the rebranding of territory has entailed an attempted regional makeover as the tourism destination of "Mesopotamia," an initiative of the Turkish GAP Regional Development Administration.[108] To be sure, the forcible orientation around the ancient past is one good way to avert discussion of more current issues such as the demolition of Kurdish homes.

But while Erdoğan is certainly well versed in the arbitrary exercise of power—such as when he spontaneously suspended daylight savings–related clock adjustments one day when I was changing planes in Istanbul and no one had the faintest clue as to what time it was—there are still

---

107 "Istanbul to change names of up to 200 streets that have Gülen-linked words." *Middle East Eye*, 14 December 2017. https://www.middleeasteye.net/news/istanbul-change-names-200-streets-have-gulen-linked-words-1060693504

108 The "Mesopotamia: Beyond a Land" website informs us that "Gap Regional Development Administration, With Tourism Oriented Promotion and Branding Project, it is aimed to increase the 'brand value" of the region through accelerating GAP region's economic, social, and cultural development [*sic*]." http://mezopotamya.travel/index.php/en/sayfa/hakkimizda]

heavily competing claims as to the identity of the Turkish homeland.[109] Many of these, however, hardly offer a more inclusive vision of Turkish society.

To pick one example off the top of my head, Mustafa of Fethiye—who resides at the bottom of the hill leading to Murat's house and with whom I've therefore come into regular contact—presides over the following worldview: Kurds are terrorists; Arabs are backstabbers who eat with their hands, smoke while they're eating, and defecate in squatting and uncivilized fashion (never mind the term "Turkish toilet"); Erdoğan is to blame for the fact that Turkish women don't sashay down the street in bikinis and that Syrian refugees are living like kings in Turkey while Turks have to make their own *rakı* to survive the oppressive alcohol tax regime; and Mustafa himself is singlehandedly to thank for the Turkish takeover of northern Cyprus in 1974. Needless to say, every available space in and around Mustafa's abode is plastered with images of Atatürk.

In the end, it might appear hypocritical of me to have abandoned one thoroughly militarized society—the United States—only to hang out in another one. But for one thing, Turkey is not a reigning global superpower specializing in the deft distribution of misery across the planet, and for another, it at least possesses a culture beyond gross overconsumption and materialism. As the *Nation* columnist and Columbia University professor Liza Featherstone once aptly put it: "I love when I'm working with nice sensitive people from other countries and they refer to 'your culture' politely as if my 'culture' is currently something other than an ongoing smelly toxic garbage fire."

---

109 "Confusion as Turkey clocks defy time-change delay." *BBC News*, 25 October 2015. https://www.bbc.com/news/world-europe-34631326

As for relations between my homeland and the Turkish one, these have as of late been in less than tip-top shape owing to a variety of factors, ranging from coup-related accusations to America's harboring of Gülen to Erdoğan's incarceration habit to differing U.S.-Turkish approaches to screwing over the Kurds in Syria. In October 2017, the *New York Times* editorial board penned "Some Urgent Questions About Turkey," a lengthy dispatch oozing characteristic imperialist condescension and laying out some of the recent transgressions of this "vital ally of the United States since World War II."

Turkey maintains the second-largest army in NATO, the *Times* reminds us, while also playing host to "military bases that are central to American operations in the Middle East, including İncirlik, where some 50 tactical nuclear weapons are stationed." When Erdoğan took over in 2003, Turkey "seemed on course to becoming a model Muslim democracy," but the Turkish president's "anti-Western behavior" has now lamentably called into question his "commitment to an alliance that is supposed to be based . . . on the common values of 'democracy, individual liberty and the rule of law.'"

The upshot of the article is that, "[g]iven Mr. Erdoğan's anti-American hostility as well as mounting security concerns, the Trump administration should give serious consideration to removing the United States nuclear weapons in Turkey"—as if it's a great privilege for the Turks to be sitting upon apocalypse-inducing materials that don't belong to them.[110] Some potentially more urgent questions might be how democracy, individual

---

110   The Editorial Board. "Some Urgent Questions About Turkey." *New York Times*, 13 October 2017. https://www.nytimes.com/2017/10/13/opinion/turkey-erdogan-nuclear-weapons.html

liberty, and the rule of law apply to the U.S. when it has the highest incarceration rate on earth and is forever bombing people.[111]

Those answers may not be forthcoming, but in the meantime there's always that penguin documentary.

111 Kann, Drew. "5 facts behind America's high incarceration rate." *CNN*, 10 July 2018. https://edition.cnn.com/2018/06/28/us/mass-incarceration-five-key-facts/index.html: "Year after year, the United States beats out much larger countries—India, China—and more totalitarian ones—Russia and the Philippines—for the distinction of having the highest incarceration rate in the world."

5. ITALY AND BEYOND

Once upon a time in Italy, a prominent citizen declared: "It is unacceptable that sometimes in certain parts of Milan there is such a presence of non Italians that instead of thinking you are in an Italian or European city, you think you are in an African city."

In case the message was not crystal clear, he then spelled it out: "Some people want a multicolored and multiethnic society. We do not share this opinion."[112]

The citizen in question was none other than Silvio Berlusconi: billionaire three-time Italian prime minister, intermittent convict, and head of a superpowerful media empire, who, as the *New York Times* put it in January 2018, has now "cleverly nurtured a constituency of aging animal lovers—and potential voters—by frequently appearing on a show on one of his networks in which he pets his fluffy white dogs and bottle-feeds lambs."[113]

---

112 For the original Italian, see "Il gran finale della campagna del Pdl Berlusconi: 'Milano sembra Africa.'" *Corriere della Sera*, 4 June 2009. https://www.corriere.it/politica/speciali/2009/elezioni/notizie/bossi_berlusconi_chiusura_campagna_elettorale_72a37414-5130-11de-9de2-00144f02aabc.shtml

113 Horowitz, Jason. "Berlusconi Is Back. Again. This Time, as Italy's 'Nonno.'" *New York Times*, 29 January 2018. https://www.nytimes.com/2018/01/29/world/europe/berlusconi-italy-election.html

Panic over the devolving color-scape of the patria is, of course, of a piece with the greater right-wing narrative of Fortress Europe, which shuns the possibility that centuries of European plunder and devastation of the African continent might have any bearing on current migration patterns. But while history lessons may not be as entertaining as lamb-nursing sessions or bunga bunga parties, it's worth noting that, in the not-so-distant past, Italians voluntarily found themselves in many African cities—and for purposes far less dignified than trying to survive.

In *The Addis Ababa Massacre: Italy's National Shame*, published by Oxford University Press, for example, author Ian Campbell explains that the Italian military occupation of Ethiopia (1936–41) was "underpinned by a policy of terror" and entailed a three-day bloodbath in February 1937 by Italian militants and civilians that wiped out—by Campbell's estimates—some 19–20 percent of the Ethiopian population of Addis Ababa.[114] A 2017 post on the Brookings Institution website furthermore recalls such highlights of Italy's colonial adventures in Libya as the internment "in a dozen concentration camps" of 10,000 or so civilians from semi-nomadic tribes.[115]

---

114 Campbell, Ian. *The Addis Ababa Massacre: Italy's National Shame.* Oxford: Oxford University Press, 2017, p. 29. It's important to remember, however, that the imperialists don't always win. In the 1896 Battle of Adwa, for example, the Italians were ignominiously defeated by the army of Ethiopia (then known as Abyssinia). Hannah Giorgis writes: "For Italy, being humiliated on the world stage by 'lesser' peoples constituted a serious blow to reputation and rank amid its Western peers. The ensuing conflicts between Italy and Ethiopia stem primarily [from] Italy's pathological need to avenge its national pride: Mussolini's 1935 invasion and subsequent occupation of Ethiopia was . . . fueled almost entirely by festering, xenophobic shame" ("If we want to understand African history, we need to understand the Battle of Adwa," *Quartz*, 11 March 2015). Ethiopia was never colonized.

115 Saini Fasanotti, Federica. "Libyans haven't forgotten history." Brookings, 18 January 2017. https://www.brookings.edu/blog/order-from-chaos/2017/01/18/libyans-havent-forgotten-history/

While the Berlusconian warning re: the creeping Africanization of Italy's northern metropolis was issued back in 2009, more recent years have also produced a deluge of xenophobic rhetoric courtesy of the Italian political élite. During an ultimately successful candidacy for the president of Lombardy in 2018, Attilio Fontana alerted Italian radio listeners to the existential threats posed by that most awful of phenomena known as immigration: "We must decide whether our ethnicity, our white race, our society should continue to exist or should be erased."[116]

This same campaign season saw Matteo Salvini—who subsequently acquired the posts of Italian interior minister and deputy prime minister— freak out about the "Islamic presence" in the country, which had resulted in a situation in which "we are under attack; at risk are our culture, society, traditions, and way of life."[117]

Credited with sounding the alarm on the Islamic attack was the late Italian journalist Oriana Fallaci, thanks to whose increased radicalization post-9/11 we learned of Muslim schemes to replace European mini-skirts with chadors and cognac with camel's milk. Excoriating U.S. universities for permitting persons named Mustafa and Muhammad to study biology and chemistry despite the danger of germ warfare, Fallaci additionally threatened in 2006 to explode a mosque and Islamic center slated for construction in Tuscany—an ironic solution, no doubt, to the issue of terrorism.[118]

---

116 In Italian: Cremonesi, Marco. "'La razza bianca rischia di sparire.' Fontana sotto accusa per la frase choc." *Corriere della Sera*, 15 January 2018. https://www.corriere.it/politica/18_gennaio_16/elezioni-2018-attilio-fontana-lega-lombardia-razza-bianca-rischia-sparire-06f0ced2-fa33-11e7-b7a0-515b75eef21a.shtml?refresh_ce-cp

117 *Ibid.*

118 For chadors, camel's milk, Mustafa, and Muhammad, see Fallaci, Oriana. "La rabbia e l'orgoglio" ["The rage and the pride"]. *Corriere della Sera*, 9 September 2006. https://www.corriere.it/

Upon assuming his offices, Salvini wasted little time getting down to business. Having pledged to deport half a million migrants as part of his vision of a "mass cleaning" of Italy—which would be carried out "street by street"—Salvini declared Italian ports closed to migrant rescue vessels, a move barely distinguishable from mass murder, given such summer 2018 headlines as "Mediterranean: more than 200 migrants drown in three days."[119]

The minister also announced plans for a census of Italy's Roma community in order to expel non-Italian members, despite reminders from human rights groups that an ethnicity-based census was not exactly legal and was furthermore reminiscent of the behavior of Benito Mussolini.[120]

Primo_Piano/Cronache/2006/09_Settembre/15/rabbia1.shtml. For the bomb threat, see Flores D'Arcais, Alberto. "Fallaci, l'ultima provocazione 'Faccio saltare la moschea in Toscana.'" *La Repubblica*, 30 May 2006. http://www.repubblica.it/2006/05/sezioni/cronaca/fallaci-moschea/ fallaci-moschea/fallaci-moschea.html. The *La Repubblica* article also includes other endearing Fallaci soundbites like: "Say you have a gun and they tell you to choose who's worse between the Muslims and the Mexicans. I'd hesitate for a second, then I'd choose the Muslims because they have broken my balls." Funnily enough, Al Giordano of *Narco News*, the outfit for which I briefly wrote from Honduras, was a great fan of Fallaci, and even mailed me one of her books in an attempt to persuade me to revise my own opinion of her. Guess it's good he resides in Mexico and not a Muslim country.

119   Kirchgaessner, Stephanie and Lorenzo Tondo and Jennifer Rankin. "Italy vows to 'send home' undocumented immigrants." *The Guardian*, 1 June 2018. https://www.theguardian.com/ world/2018/jun/01/italy-vows-to-send-home-undocumented-immigrants; Giuffrida, Angela. "Italy's first black senator: my election shows far-right is not anti-immigration." *The Guardian*, 8 March 2018. https://www.theguardian.com/world/2018/mar/08/italys-first-black-senator- my-election-shows-far-right-is-not-anti-immigration; "Migrant crisis: Italy minister Salvini closes ports to NGO boats." *BBC News*, 30 June 2018. https://www.bbc.com/news/world-eu- rope-44668062; Wintour, Patrick. "Mediterranean: more than 200 migrants drown in three days." *The Guardian*, 3 July 2018. https://www.theguardian.com/world/2018/jul/03/mediterra- nean-migrants-drown-three-days-libya-italy

120   Embury-Dennis, Tom. "Italy's deputy PM Salvini called for 'mass cleansing, street by street, quar- ter by quarter,' newly resurfaced footage reveals." *The Independent*, 21 June 2018. https://www .independent.co.uk/news/world/europe/italy-matteo-salvini-video-immigration-mass-cleans- ing-roma-travellers-far-right-league-party-a8409506.html

I, on the other hand, continue to be permitted access to Italian territory any which way I please on account of my own acceptable skin color and passport, an arrangement that has enabled me to spend a part of each summer in the southern region of Puglia without risking maritime death or street-cleaning.

So, too, has it offered me a glimpse of the frontline in the great battle for Italian culture and homeland in the face of camel's milk and similar plots.

* * *

My inaugural visit to Puglia took place in the summer of 2004, when Amelia and I briefly parted ways after our first round of avocado packing in Spain and doing nothing much of anything in Turkey. A boy named Gianluca from the town of Oria in the heel of the Italian boot—with whom I was conducting a not-extremely-scrupulous long-distance relationship based on approximately two encounters—invited me to his territory while Amelia paid her annual visit to the U.S. to avert the confiscation of her Green Card. Though our relationship was eventually officially downgraded to friendship, it was made clear that I was still part of the family and would forevermore be force-fed as such.

Gianluca's father had passed away some years before, leaving Gianluca's mother Adriana to care for *la nonnina*—her mother-in-law—who by the time I entered the picture already spent most of the day confined to the bed yet still managed periodic shrieks, lest anyone in the vicinity become too comfortable. Other attention-generating methods included hallucinating a string of lovers in hot pursuit of Adriana and shouting for the priest, as well as halfheartedly attempting suicide with household items ranging from a hammer to a window curtain. In each case, crisis resolution took the form of the usual barrage of Italian penis- and testicle-centric curse words, followed by yet another plate of pasta slammed down in front of *la nonnina*.

Located just east of Taranto and half an hour from the Ionian Sea, Oria is organized around a castle built by crusader and Holy Roman Emperor Frederick II. Legend has it that the town owes its continued existence to a benevolent intervention by Saint Barsanofio, who summoned cloud cover one fine day during World War II and thereby thwarted a planned bombing raid.

In keeping with the Italian tradition of evacuating the cities for the coast in times of infernal heat, Adriana & Co. moved each summer to her plot of land by the sea, which features a small house off a dirt lane. Off the same dirt lane are the respective summertime abodes of Adriana's four siblings. Olive trees and grapevines abound. The address, as far as I have been able to determine, is: "Turn left after the twelfth utility pole after the first bridge on the main road leading from the closest seaside hamlet."

When *la nonnina* ultimately perished of natural causes and Gianluca and his brothers—all of whom lived elsewhere in Italy—curtailed their visits to Puglia, I ended up with my own room at the beach house, where I spent many summer nights partaking of one-euro liters of wine and serving as captive audience to Italian homicide TV shows, opiate of the Italian masses. Supplementary entertainment was provided by a steady stream of visiting relatives, each of them committed to sustaining an ambience of cacophonous drama and well versed in the art of Italo-gesticulation, thanks to which even the most banal of discussions about inflatable mattresses or plastic cups became a lively spectacle.

One recurring theme, to be sure, was migration, about which everyone was pretty much in consensus but nonetheless still needed to shout about. Initially, migrants were often referred to collectively as *marocchini*—which could apply to anyone from Morocco to Sudan to Bangladesh—and blamed for creating all manner of trouble in *casa nostra* when they should have stayed put in *casa loro*. Shot down were all attempts by me to interject details about real live *marocchini*—such as Abdul, who had hosted Amelia and me for numerous months in southern Spain; Abdul's family, who had hosted us in Morocco itself; and the surplus of Moroccans who had picked us up hitchhiking and were in fact generally the only demographic that picked us up in Spain aside from intoxicated Spaniards returning from the disco on weekend mornings.

As the Puglian discourse grew more sophisticated over the years, Italy-bound refugees and migrants graduated from being uniformly Moroccan but remained uniformly viewed as thieves, rapists, and killers—though proof of such behavior was never forthcoming. Another common complaint had to do with the notion that hard-earned taxpayer money was being flung at each and every individual who happened to wash up on Italian shores, to be squandered on luxury hotel accommodations, the latest cell phones, and whatever other goodies the lazy and opportunistic refugee heart might desire.

Obviously, the channeling of public attention and wrath toward the "Other" is a handy distraction from institutionalized corruption in Italy, whereby members of the ruling class fling hard-earned taxpayer money at themselves. And the process is rendered all the more fluid when the media is dutifully standing by to provide the proper talking points.

Consider an item on the website of Italy's *Il Giornale* newspaper—published by Berlusconi's very own brother, who in 2016 valiantly defended the paper's decision to distribute copies of *Mein Kampf*—advising that "Italy IS NOT an Islamic country," despite the best attempts of "he who invades me trying to expel me from my land" and "he who wants to take me a thousand years back to when the Moors landed . . . on my shores to rape and kill."[121]

As is the case in U.S. propaganda starring Muslims and Mexicans as invaders, rapists, and murderers, the decisive Western monopoly on destructive activity in the opposite direction is conveniently lost in the equation. Afghanistan and Iraq come to mind, where U.S.-led kill-fests boasting Italian participation have not in the least bit mitigated presumptions of the inviolable sanctity of U.S. and Italian borders, respectively.

In my meanderings through Italy, I have inevitably come across some of the miscreants intent on sabotaging the chromatic composition of the Italian homeland. In 2015, I spoke with a 20-something-year-old Eritrean migrant in Rome who went by the name of Jerry and who had fled his own torture-prone homeland two years previously, thus extricating himself from eternal military service.

While Italy had of course felt no qualms about helping itself to the colony of Eritrea back in the day, Jerry quickly assumed the position of *persona non grata* alongside his fellow itinerant Eritreans in Rome, where he had taken up residence in an abandoned office building near the city's central

---

121 See Spirlì, Nino. "L'Italia NON è un Paese islamico." *Il Giornale* (blog), 3 August 2015. http://blog.ilgiornale.it/spirli/2015/08/03/litalia-non-e-un-paese-islamico/?repeat=w3tc, and "Milano, Paolo Berlusconi difende l'operazione 'Mein Kampf': 'Razionale e ragionevole.'" *La Repubblica*, 12 June 2016. https://milano.repubblica.it/cronaca/2016/06/12/news/paolo_berlusconi-141880718/?refresh_ce

train station (i.e. the luxury accommodations detected by the Puglians) and had begun offering informal English lessons as a means of not starving.

Reflecting on whether or not it had been worth it to risk his life traveling from Eritrea to Ethiopia to Sudan to the migrant torture-rape-kidnapping-slavery hotspot of Libya—spending three weeks in the desert and then four days crossing the Mediterranean in a storm while trapped in a tiny vessel with 300 other people—Jerry concluded that, in terms of hope for the future, he was still pretty much where he had started.[122]

Also in Rome in 2015, I paid a visit to the Baobab center in the Tiburtino neighborhood, which catered primarily to Eritrean migrants transiting to northern Europe. Although designed to shelter fewer than 200 people, the center was reportedly often packed to over four times its capacity. On the day of my visit, the guests included a sobbing young woman who had just been informed that her brother had been kidnapped while attempting his own migration.

The following year, I again found myself among uprooted Eritreans, this time many thousands of kilometers away, in a refugee camp in Ethiopia, another country my passport and I were able to access with incredible ease—since just because Africans had to jump through lethal hoops to exit their continent didn't mean white people shouldn't be able to go on safari at the drop of a hat. I myself did not undertake any activities involving wildlife, although I did visit the Addis Ababa tomb of Ethiopia's last emperor, Haile Selassie, as well as consume an inordinate quantity of pineapple pizza. My Lebanese boyfriend was also in attendance, but was posing

---

122 Farand, Chloe. "Refugees face kidnap, torture, rape and slavery in Libyan 'living hell,' Oxfam report says." *The Independent*, 9 August 2017. https://www.independent.co.uk/news/world/europe/refugees-kidnap-torture-rape-slavery-libya-living-hell-oxfam-medu-borderline-siciliar-eport-a7883346.html

as a Venezuelan in light of Lebanon's notoriety in the region as a living hell for Ethiopian and other migrant domestic workers.[123]

From Addis we embarked on a two-day bus ride north. Acquiring bus tickets was almost as much of an adventure as the trip itself given the intricacies of the Ethiopian calendar—according to which it was then 2008—and the timekeeping system, according to which, if it was 10 a.m. everywhere else in the East Africa Time Zone, it was 4 a.m. in Ethiopia.

In the northern Ethiopian town of Shire, not far from the Eritrean border, I had an arbitrary acquaintance in the form of an Irish freelance journalist I had met the previous year at a conference in Tehran to which I had accidentally been invited. This dapper gentleman was married to an Ethiopian woman, delighted by his purchasing power in Ethiopian birr, and, it seemed, the talk of the town (for an approximate visual, think Willy Wonka in Africa).

He kindly introduced us to the prime beer-drinking spots in Shire as well as to an American representative of a European humanitarian NGO operating

---

123   See Fernández, Belén. "Lebanon's maid trade is modified slavery." *Al Jazeera America*, 26 March 2015.   http://america.aljazeera.com/opinions/2015/3/lebanons-maid-trade-is-modified-slavery.html In which I visited housemaid recruitment agencies in Beirut pretending to be in the market for a domestic worker. At the House of Maids agency I was received by one Khaled Shmaitelly, who informed me that live-in Ethiopian and Kenyan maids came with a monthly price-tag of $200, while Bangladeshis were paid $150. Ethiopians without knowledge of English or Arabic also got the Bangladeshi fee. "When I asked in my best whine if I was required to give the maid a day off, Shmaitelly assured me I was not, though Kenyans and Ethiopians are allowed to phone home once every 15 days. If my maid proved defective within the first three months, he would exchange her for free." The confiscation of maids' passports and the frequency of physical and emotional abuse by employers has resulted in a situation in which it's not uncommon in Lebanon to hear of young domestic workers plunging off of balconies to their deaths. Then again, god forbid the élite Lebanese have to carry their own shopping bags or raise their own children.

in the town, who confirmed that his organization was actually receiving big bucks from ultra-right-wing European entities concerned with curbing the northward flow of refugees and migrants. Humanitarian, indeed.

While the NGO-er insisted that I'd never be granted authorization to enter the Hitsats refugee camp—located in a desolate area about an hour from Shire—the obstacles proved not so insurmountable, and my boyfriend and I were escorted there one afternoon by the proprietor of our hotel, where we were the only guests and which may or may not have been a money-laundering front.

The proprietor was a middle-aged Sudanese man who explained to us that he had gone from being an orphan in Khartoum to being a driver in Saudi Arabia for some component of the royal family to striking it rich with the help of his Saudi patron, who had suggested that he invest in gold. What business he may have been contemplating in Hitsats was never revealed, but he took a number of photographs of a small church rising from the heat and dust, where we stopped to chat with a group of barefoot refugees, some of them sporting Eritrea soccer shirts, as they went about painting the façade of the structure.

One member of the group outlined his own reasons for fleeing Eritrea, which, as with Jerry in Rome, had to do with forcible and unending military service that was tantamount to slavery. Following eight years of army life and no end in sight, the man had escaped to Ethiopia in 2015 and had yet to communicate with his mother, whom he feared had been punished for his transgressions. He had now entered into indefinite limbo in Hitsats, lacking the funds for onward travel. The cheapest price tag he'd heard for being smuggled to Greece, he said, was around $5,000—i.e. over nine times the per capita annual income in Ethiopia at the time, according to the World Bank's calculations.

By coincidence, around the same time that I was visiting Hitsats, Thomas Friedman had also descended upon Africa to explain things about migration. This was a continent he rarely managed to visit, despite his self-declared unlimited travel budget courtesy of the *New York Times*. The occasional previous descent had enabled such impressive journalistic feats as a 121-word description of a leopard eating an antelope in a Botswanan tree in 2009.[124]

Predictably titled "Out of Africa" and "Out of Africa, Part II," Friedman's April 2016 intervention took him to "the headwaters of the immigration flood now flowing from Africa to Europe via Libya," which—along with the "refugees fleeing wars in Syria, Iraq and Afghanistan"—had created "two flows pos[ing] a huge challenge for the future of Europe." The upshot, in Friedman's view, was that "we have to help [the Africans] fix their gardens because no walls will keep them home."[125]

While the average innocent reader may have been hard-pressed to determine how the gardening solution factored into the picture when gardens were not mentioned anywhere else in the two-part series, it goes without saying that someone who has devoted his life to promoting the capitalist destruction of the globe is not exactly the most qualified candidate for African gardener. It furthermore bears reiterating that Friedman had also valiantly championed the very refugee-producing wars now challenging the "future of Europe."

---

124 Friedman, Thomas. "The Land of 'No Service.'" *New York Times*, 15 August 2009. https://www.nytimes.com/2009/08/16/opinion/16friedman.html

125 "Out of Africa." *New York Times*, 13 April 2016. https://www.nytimes.com/2016/04/13/opinion/out-of-africa.html; "Out of Africa, Part II." *New York Times*, 20 April 2016. http://www.nytimes.com/2016/04/20/opinion/out-of-africa-part-ii.html?smid=tw-tomfriedman&smtyp=cur&_r=0

As journalist and author Matt Taibbi once commented with regard to Friedman's schizophrenic bid to reinvent himself as an environmentalist:

> Where does a man who needs his own offshore drilling platform just to keep the east wing of his house heated get the balls to write a book chiding America for driving energy inefficient automobiles? Where does a guy whose family bulldozed 2.1 million square feet of pristine Hawaiian wilderness to put a Gap, an Old Navy, a Sears, an Abercrombie and even a motherfucking Foot Locker in paradise get off preaching to the rest of us about the need for a "Green Revolution"?[126]

Moral of the story: perhaps Friedman should focus on fixing his own garden first.

* * *

In the meantime, the African garden has produced plenty of tales of rootlessness and exile far less frivolous in nature than my own.

In the Maltese town of Birżebbuġa in 2014, for example, I made the acquaintance of a young Gambian man by the last name of Manneh, who, like many migrants, had ended up on the island of Malta by accident while trying to reach Italy by sea. Facing a lack of sustainable employment options at home, Manneh had slowly made his way from Gambia to Libya and then boarded a small vessel with more than 120 other people to cross the Mediterranean.

Four days later the passengers had run out of food and water and the boat had acquired a leak, at which point it was intercepted by a U.S. warship,

---

126   See Finnegan Bungeroth, Megan. "Flat N All That: Matt Taibbi Eviscerates Thomas Friedman's 'Hot, Flat, and Crowded.'" *NY Press*, 14 January 2009. http://www.nypress.com/flat-n-all-that/

which handed the human cargo off to the Maltese. In keeping with Malta's policy of mandatory detention of migrants, Manneh was interned for several months at the Safi detention center, located on an army base; in case there remained any doubt about his fundamentally criminal identity, even visits to the hospital required him to be put in handcuffs.

Offering to accompany me by public bus to the nearby Maltese capital of Valletta, Manneh pointed out key landmarks such as the so-called immigration reception center near Birżebbuġa where he had been transferred once it had been decided that he no longer needed to be detained full-time. At the center he slept in a small trailer referred to as a "container" with seven other persons. He drew attention to cement pipes situated around the establishment's perimeter, inside which migrants who had been expelled from the center had taken up residence.

Human rights lawyer Neil Falzon, director of the Malta-based human rights foundation Aditus, speculated that the reason Malta insisted on implementing what he described as "the most expensive, forceful, and harmful migration management regime" had to do with the government's "need to be perceived as a strong and controlling force." He told me that the fanatical detention scheme, which didn't even spare young children, was presented to the Maltese public as necessary for "national security [and] social order" and was justified via regular "reminders of invasion, terrorism, disease, and over-population."

Indeed, the government's approach seemed to have paid off, as another Gambian I met in Birżebbuġa reported having nearly had the police called on him for daring to say hello to someone in the street. Of course, other varieties of foreigner were more than welcome in Malta—such as those to whom the government was then aiming to sell European Union passports for 1.15 million euros a pop.[127]

Like Italy, Malta has expended much energy whining about its disproportionate refugee burden and endeavoring to wrest the role of victim from the refugees themselves. But while European governments exempt themselves from humanitarian standards by arguing that intimidating refugees in fact helps save lives by deterring migration, intimidation is ineffective when people have nothing to lose. And as long as the prevailing economic system depends upon borders that apply to have-nots but not to predatory corporations or the ubiquitous U.S. military, migration patterns will hold.

In 2015, I visited some of the informal tented settlements for Syrian refugees in Lebanon's Bekaa Valley. There, an older Syrian man from the city of Homs noted that an increasing number of young people in his camp were trying their luck with what he called the "boats of death" to Europe—his two sons included, from whom he'd had no news since they'd departed Lebanon. The risks of this passage were immaterial, he said, because the refugees saw themselves as essentially dead already. Another group of Syrians responded to the question of how they envisioned the future by placing their hands over their eyes: "We cannot see anything."

On my annual summer excursion to Puglia in 2018, the Italians had amassed more trivia re: the migrant scourge. They filled me in one evening around the plastic table on Adriana's patio near the coast, where an assortment of relatives gathered amidst the deafening song of the

---

127 Gittleson, Kim. "Where is the cheapest place to buy citizenship?" *BBC News*, 4 June 2014. https://www.bbc.com/news/business-27674135

cicadas and a swarm of repellent-resistant mosquitoes. Once the usual topics had been covered—the malevolent euro, the geriatric cousin whose savings were being rapidly appropriated by a much-younger seductress, the thieving *bastardo* poultry vendor in a neighboring village whose hens refused to lay eggs, the three Neapolitans who had disappeared in Mexico and become instant stars-in-absentia of the Italian TV homicide programs—it was the migrants' turn. Thanks to the ensuing raucous symposium, conducted half in Italian and half in dialect, I learned that the Italian *governo di merda* had stooped to new lows in its obsequiousness vis-à-vis Italy's foreign guests, who were now getting steak feasts while the native population was forced to survive on tomatoes and bread.

Following a brief detour into a debate over whether tomatoes and bread might not in fact be preferable as well as reminiscent of the good old postwar days when life was much simpler, the *governo di merda* was unanimously proclaimed to have become less *merda* with the ascension that year of minister Salvini, vanquisher of migrants, Roma, and whatever other Others might be lurking.

Salvini, incidentally, was also the head of the political party known until recently as the *Lega Nord*—Northern League—before the "Northern" qualifier was dropped to accommodate right-wing maniacs in central and southern Italy, as well. Given the traditional disdain in the more prosperous and organized Italian north for anything southern, the potential for nationwide solidarity in the face of the refugee assault was no doubt heartening.

My Puglian interlocutors were additionally sympathetic to the border battle being fought in my own homeland, and concluded that—as had been demonstrated by the fate of the Neapolitans—Mexicans were obviously also criminals.

*   *   *

In May 2017, I took an overnight ferry from the Italian port of Civitavecchia to the Tunisian capital of Tunis to see my American friend Max, who was in the process of extending for as long as conceivably possible his PhD research. The Civitavecchia-Tunis ferry was preceded by an overnight Barcelona-Civitavecchia ferry, during which I slept in a chair in a large room with various Muslims intent on destroying Europe from within by playing the call to prayer on their cell phones. Also on board was a horde of Spanish high school students conducting an interminable dance party on the deck, on account of which experience I definitively entered misanthropic old age.

The second ferry contained a parasitic Italian who was en route to a seaside resort in Hammamet because Tunis was too smelly. He wagged his finger at me upon learning that Lebanon was my post-Tunisia destination: "*È rischioso.*" I eventually disentangled myself from his company and relocated to the cafeteria, where a Tunisian man promptly pitched his blanket next to my table and offered me water, soda, canned sardines, and aspirin—in other words, all of the ingestible materials he had on hand. Having manically stockpiled wine at the port, I was already set.

The man was on his way home for a visit from the northern Italian city of Ancona, where he had worked in a plastic factory for the past 15 years. At first he was upbeat about everything—Ancona, plastic, sardines—but then he confessed to me that he often questioned his decision to abandon his village near the Tunisian-Algerian border for the economic temptations of Italy, where, he declared, there was little proper food to be found, contrary to popular belief.

In the village his family grew everything necessary for human nutrition and happiness, he said, as he launched into a crash course on the beauty of bread-making. For his wife and three children, who continued to reside in the village year-round, he was bearing gifts of motor scooters and kitchen equipment, all packed into his Fiat Panda aboard the ferry. He inquired after my own marital status and pronounced himself overjoyed that my *ragazzo* was Arab.

The theme of food sovereignty would come up again when Max and I flew to the Tunisian island of Djerba to rendezvous with his comrade Habib Ayeb, a Tunisian geographer, academic, and documentary filmmaker based at the University of Paris VIII in France. The first attempt at takeoff by the notorious Tunisair ended when the plane careened down the runway only to execute a 180-degree turn and arrive back at the terminal. We dismounted and were loaded onto another plane, this one by the name of Hannibal.

The receiving line at the tiny Djerba airport included a surplus of heavily armed black-clad men in balaclavas, a testament in part to Tunisia's ISIS problem—which, to be sure, was nothing that couldn't be resolved with a little military assistance from the United States, a.k.a. the very entity that had assisted the rise of ISIS in the first place.[128] Additional U.S.

---

128 The existence of Al Qaeda in Iraq, a precursor to ISIS, is a direct result of the U.S. invasion in 2003. In addition to setting the whole terror-ball rolling, the U.S. also made more specific contributions to the rise of ISIS, such as detaining countless Iraqis, "many of them noncombatants"— Mehdi Hasan notes at *The Intercept*—"at Camp Bucca in southern Iraq, where imprisoned

contributions to the Tunisian homeland became apparent as Ayeb showed us around Djerba and other sections of southern Tunisia, providing politico economic interpretations of the striking landscape.

Despite the overabundance of olive orchards and the centrality of olive oil to the Tunisian diet, Ayeb lamented, the substance had become prohibitively expensive for many families. Luckily, the American outfit euphemistically known as USAID was on hand as usual to endow the suffering of the developing world with a façade of progress. As of the summer of 2017, the top "success story" on the USAID website's Tunisia page was a short report from 2013 titled "Tunisian olive oil finds a new gourmet market," celebrating the attendance of eleven Tunisian olive oil companies at New York's Fancy Food Show that year.[129]

This mind-blowing success was naturally attributed to USAID itself, which in the aftermath of Tunisia's revolution of 2010-11 "began working with

---

jihadis were able to not only radicalize new recruits in plain sight, but also plan future operations and attacks" ("Blowback: How ISIS was created by the U.S. invasion of Iraq," 29 January 2018. https://theintercept.com/2018/01/29/isis-iraq-war-islamic-state-blowback/). A number of men who would go on to become top ISIS commanders served time there. To be sure, invading, occupying, slaughtering, and imprisoning is a pretty good way to ensure a steady stream of enemies for the foreseeable future. In a 2015 *Guardian* piece titled "Now the truth emerges: how the U.S. fuelled the rise of Isis in Syria and Iraq," meanwhile, Seumas Milne discussed a declassified U.S. intelligence report indicating that, "a year into the Syrian rebellion, the U.S. and its allies weren't only supporting and arming an opposition they knew to be dominated by extreme sectarian groups; they were prepared to countenance the creation of some sort of 'Islamic state'—despite the 'grave danger' to Iraq's unity—as a Sunni buffer to weaken Syria" (3 June 2015, https://www.theguardian.com/commentisfree/2015/jun/03/us-isis-syria-iraq). Of course, as with every other problem it has helped to create, the U.S. also fancied itself qualified to preside over the "solution" to ISIS, which naturally entailed more bombs.

129 "Tunisian olive oil finds a new gourmet market." Now viewable as archived content on the USAID website: https://2012-2017.usaid.gov/results-data/success-stories/tunisian-olive-oil-finds-new-gourmet-market

local [Tunisian] partners on a broad range of economic development programs to address some of the underlying causes of the revolution: high
unemployment, lack of opportunities, and barriers to economic growth."
And *voilà*, the miraculous one-step solution to socioeconomic inequality
and all other ailments: a gourmet export market that actively prevents poor
people from consuming the things that grow on their land.

Ayeb's 2017 documentary *Couscous: Seeds of Dignity* further exposes
corporate-capitalist agricultural policies in Tunisia that obliterate any
prospect of food sovereignty under the guise of "development." In the
film, Tunisian farmers speak with eloquence, humor, and dignified rage
on such subjects as the calamitous invasion of imported seed varieties that
proved far less resilient than local ones and resulted in subpar harvests,
diminishing flavor and nutritional value, and a proliferation of seeds with
nonrenewable traits—i.e. ones that can't be replanted and must instead be
continually repurchased from the supplier. So much for sustainability.

Also spotlighted is the toxic reliance on imported pesticides and chemicals
required for the maintenance of non-indigenous seeds. One especially ani-
mated character—named, as irony would have it, Eisenhower—denounces
"the West's strategy" to dominate markets, to keep Tunisia "ever under
their heel," and in fact to "kill our agriculture." Eisenhower's verb choice
would appear to be particularly appropriate given the track record of
Western agribusiness deities like the U.S. biotech giant Monsanto, which
has undertaken the task of dousing the planet with its signature herbicide
Roundup while also presiding over country-specific feats like helping to
set off an Indian farmer suicide epidemic (speaking of killing, prior to its
reinvention as a "sustainable agriculture company," Monsanto served as
Vietnam war-era manufacturer of the lethal defoliant Agent Orange).[130]

---

130 In the case of India, the takeover of farmland by Monsanto's Bacillus thuringiensis (Bt) cotton—
     which promised increased crop yields and resilience to pests—in fact drove countless farm-
     ers into insuperable debt. Between 1995 and 2012, nearly 300,000 farmers committed suicide

And while the West purports to hold the keys to the future, it's also intent on perpetuating the past; as scholar Corinna Mullin, then a visiting assistant professor at the University of Tunis, remarked to me, Tunisia's post-colonial period happened to entail "many structural continuities with the forms of accumulation and dispossession that characterized French colonial rule," which ended in 1956.

Nowadays, she said, continuity is "manifested in ongoing forms of extractivism" that have been encouraged and facilitated "by international

---

(see Borromeo, Leah. "Why are Indian farmers committing suicide over their debts?" *New Statesman*, 27 November 2012. https://www.newstatesman.com/world-affairs/2012/11/why-are-indian-farmers-committing-suicide-over-their-debts). In 2013, renowned Indian physicist and author Vandana Shiva noted that field studies in the region of Vidarbha indicated "a 13 fold increase in use of pesticides after Bt cotton was introduced" (in tragic irony, these very pesticides have constituted the suicide weapon of choice for many farmers). Shiva furthermore observed: "GMOs are intrinsically linked to Intellectual Property Rights, which in turn are linked to royalty payments. Royalties are extracted from poor farmers through credit and debt . . . The shift to Bt cotton meant a jump of 8000% in the cost of seed" (Shiva, Vandana. "Seed monopolies, GMOs, and farmer suicides in India – a response to Nature," 12 November 2013. Article accessible via the website of GM Watch: https://www.gmwatch.org/en/news/archive/2013/15165-vandana-shiva-on-seed-monopolies-gmos-and-farmer-suicides-in-india). And what do you know: the global predations of Monsanto and similar companies are facilitated by none other than the U.S. government (see, for example, Gillam, Carey. "UPDATE 1-U.S. State Dept. promotes Monsanto's GMO crops overseas – report." *Reuters*, 14 May 2013. https://www.reuters.com/article/usa-gmo-report/update-1-u-s-state-dept-promotes-monsanto-gmo-crops-overseas-report-idUSL2N0DV2XF20130514). For the legacy of Agent Orange in Vietnam, meanwhile, see the *Al Jazeera* documentary *Children of Agent Orange*, which explores the "strong evidence that the deadly dioxins . . . had a catastrophic effect on the health of millions of Vietnamese – killing hundreds of thousands and causing dreadful diseases and birth defects in subsequent generations right up to this day" (28 September 2011, https://www.aljazeera.com/programmes/peopleandpower/2011/09/2011928111920665336.html). Nowadays, Monsanto fits right in with the capitalist modus operandi of extracting profit by poisoning the earth, and is only rarely made to answer for its transgressions—as when Dewayne Johnson, a terminally ill Californian, was awarded $78 million (down from an original $289) in a landmark lawsuit against the company. A former school groundskeeper, Johnson claimed that Roundup was the cause of his cancer. (Yan, Holly. "Cancer patient who was awarded $289 million in Monsanto trial says he'll take $78 million instead." *CNN*, 1 November 2018. https://edition.cnn.com/2018/11/01/health/monsanto-plaintiff-accepts-lower-award/index.html. The article specified, however, that Bayer—the company that recently acquired Monsanto—would appeal the verdict.)

financial institutions, the EU, the U.S. and other prominent (neo)coloni-al-capitalist actors" concerned with pushing "neoliberal 'development' . . . for the benefit of international and a segment of local capital."

In our final stop before returning to Tunis, Ayeb accompanied Max and me to the southern coastal city of Gabès, a hub of corporate exploitation that boasts the world's only—rapidly dwindling—coastal oasis as well as the distinction of being Tunisia's cancer capital.[131] Presumably, this has something to do with the city's industrial zone, which comprises phosphate refineries and other poisonous for-export operations that have been known to generate "clouds of rotten-smelling yellow gas" as well as tons of radio-active waste dumped into the sea.[132]

The three of us stayed the night in Gabès at a home shared by several broth-ers and their families, who arranged cushions for us on the cement floor and served up a colossal mound of couscous. One of the children, a girl not yet two years old, was covered from head to toe in splotchy rashes that her parents said had been written off as "normal" by each of the four doctors that had been consulted—another casualty, perhaps, of killer development models.

The next morning, our drive back to Tunis was accompanied by a tyran-nical wind that caused trash and dust to fly and swirl around the vehicle. Before Ayeb had the chance to name the phenomenon, I recognized it from Italy: the *scirocco*, defined by *Encyclopedia Britannica* as "a hot, very humid,

131 Lageman, Thessa. "Is help on the way for Tunisia's cancer hotspot?" *Al Jazeera*, 29 December 2015. https://www.aljazeera.com/news/2015/12/tunisia-cancer-hotspot-151213062057351.html

132 See Kimball, Sam. "Phosphate production poisoning Tunisian city." *Al-Monitor*, 22 January, 2015. https://www.al-monitor.com/pulse/originals/2015/01/tunisia-gabes-mineral-produc-tion-employment-pollution.html; "Pollution in Gabes, Tunisia's shore of death." *Al Jazeera*, 14 June 2013. https://www.aljazeera.com/indepth/features/2013/06/20136913247297963.html

and oppressive wind, blow[ing] frequently from Africa and the Middle East." Indeed, one could always tell the onset of the *scirocco* in Puglia by a feeling of massive stupidity and agitation—not to mention the desire to suspend one's entire existence until the wind had blown its course.

In a world defined by borders, it seems oppressive winds know none.

6. ONWARD

Not everywhere in the world, of course, rolls out the red carpet for a U.S. passport. Some countries make the entitled American traveler work for the luxury of cross-border movement.

My visa for Uzbekistan, for example, required a moderate amount of hoop-jumping as well as a minor nervous breakdown at the Uzbek consulate in Istanbul, which I managed to locate by chance given that its staff, when contacted by telephone, professed not to know the current address. I eventually landed in the capital city of Tashkent, where the Uzbek subway police kept me on my toes by continuously requesting my passport as well as the slip of paper certifying that my presence in the country had been registered with the Ministry of Internal Affairs. Occasionally, pertinent supplementary information was also requested, such as why a woman of my age had not yet reproduced.

Not far to the south of Uzbekistan, a certain centerpiece of the "Axis of Evil" also justifiably exercises great caution when admitting citizens of the Great Satan—hence my utter glee when, in the summer of 2015, I discovered in my email an invitation to a conference in Tehran on the subject of Iranian victims of terrorism. The sole complicating factor was that the invite was addressed not to me but to General Mirza Aslam Beg, the former commander of the armed forces of Pakistan.

Concentrated harassment of the conference organizers resulted in my very own invitation, followed by weeks of visa negotiations and a frantic trip to the Iranian embassy in Madrid. At last I found myself on a plane bound for the Islamic Republic along with Jorge Verstrynge, a reformed Spanish fascist politician who had later served as a military adviser to Hugo Chávez and was scheduled as a conference speaker, until it was revealed upon arrival at Imam Khomeini airport that he did not possess the requisite command of English. The language barrier proved auspicious indeed as Verstrynge promptly announced in Spanish that Iran and Israel were natural allies—which they surely had been in the good old prerevolutionary days, when the Israelis helped train the shah's homicidal secret police force.

Among Verstrynge's numerous other opinions, some of which he had taken the liberty of dictating to the Iranian ambassador to Spain, was that Iran was in dire need of a nuclear weapon. This particular idea, he said, had been politely shot down as contradictory to religious policy. To be sure, the fluidity of the U.S.-Israeli-backed narrative—whereby a hellbent nuclear Iran is plotting the demise of life as we know it—is beset by plenty of inopportune facts on the ground, including that the U.S. built Iran's first nuclear reactor in 1967 and, as NPR notes, "provided Iran with fuel for that reactor—weapons-grade enriched uranium."[133] The *Washington Post* reminds us that, in the 1970s, "the [Gerald] Ford administration—in which [Dick] Cheney succeeded [Donald] Rumsfeld] as chief of staff and [Paul] Wolfowitz was responsible for nonproliferation issues at the Arms Control

---

133 Inskeep, Steve. "Born In The USA: How America Created Iran's Nuclear Program." NPR, 18 September 2015. https://www.npr.org/sections/parallels/2015/09/18/440567960/born-in-the-u-s-a-how-america-created-irans-nuclear-program?t=1532699193772

and Disarmament Agency—continued intense efforts to supply Iran with U.S. nuclear technology."[134] In subsequent years, these same characters felt themselves qualified to lead the battle against Iran's alleged nuclear ambitions.

At the conference I spoke with Shohreh Pirani, the widow of Dariush Rezaeinejad, an academic and deputy at the Atomic Energy Organization of Iran assassinated in 2011. The killing was witnessed by Pirani and the couple's young daughter, who, now eight years old, instructed her mother on the matter of which family photos to show me on the cell phone. I also spoke with the father of Mostafa Ahmadi Roshan, who had worked at the Natanz Fuel Enrichment Plant prior to his death by magnetic car bomb in 2012 at the age of 32.

According to his father, Ahmadi Roshan had labored under the conviction that a peaceful nuclear program would help ensure Iranian sovereignty—a word that naturally doesn't mesh with the logic of imperialism. In February 2012, NBC presented the following headline with regard to the assassination pattern: "Israel teams with terror group to kill Iran's nuclear scientists, U.S. officials tell NBC News."[135] Later that year, the "terror group" in question—the Mujahedin-e Khalq (MEK), a violent regime change cult—was conveniently delisted as a terrorist organization by the U.S., which was good news for John Bolton, Rudy Giuliani, and other high-profile Americans who would go on to collect obscene amounts of money in exchange for tripping

134 Linzer, Dafna. "Past Arguments Don't Square With Current Iran Policy." *Washington Post*, 27 March 2015. http://www.washingtonpost.com/wp-dyn/articles/A3983-2005Mar26.html

135 Engel, Richard and Robert Windrem, 9 February 2012. http://rockcenter.nbcnews.com/_news/2012/02/08/10354553-israel-teams-with-terror-group-to-kill-irans-nuclear-scientists-us-officials-tell-nbc-news

over themselves in praise of the rehabilitated terrorists.[136] Israel, for its part, continued to preside over a gigantic "secret" nuclear arsenal, estimated by many to contain between 80 and 200 nuclear warheads—weapons that exist in contravention of the very nonproliferation treaty trotted out to justify the punishment of Iran.[137] Never mind, too, the suggestion by U.S. intelligence itself that the Islamic Republic halted nuclear weapons efforts in 2003.[138]

In 2016, I returned on my own to Iran for a two-week stint in the architectural gem of Esfahan. This was preceded by a months-long visa process overseen by an Iranian travel agent who agreed to circumvent the government's mandatory ever-present-guide rule for citizens of the Great

---

136 For the official delisting, see "Delisting of the Mujahedin-e Khalq," U.S. State Department website, 28 September 2012. https://www.state.gov/j/ct/rls/other/des/266607.htm. Not that the group didn't enjoy relative freedom of movement beforehand; as Trita Parsi points out at *The New York Review of Books*, the terror-listed MEK's "office was in the National Press Club building [and] its Norooz receptions on Capitol Hill were well attended by lawmakers and Hill staff alike." Parsi also references reports that Bolton in particular receives "as much as $180,000 for his appearances at the group's events" ("Why Trump's Hawks Back the MEK Terrorist Cult," 20 July 2018. https://www.nybooks.com/daily/2018/07/20/why-trumps-hawks-back-the-mek-terrorist-cult/). While the MEK has practically no support whatsoever within Iran on account of its alliance with Saddam Hussein in the Iran-Iraq War and its numerous attacks and assassinations on Iranian soil, the cult is hailed by influential members of the Trump administration as a democratic solution and "the vision for the future of Iran"—as Giuliani put it in one of his own heavily compensated speeches (see Hilsum, Lindsey. "The shadowy cult Trump advisors tout as an alternative to the Iranian government." Channel 4 News, 6 September 2018. https://www.channel4.com/news/the-shadowy-cult-trump-advisors-tout-as-an-alternative-to-the-iranian-government). Never mind that it's not clear what sort of future is logistically possible in light of the MEK's mandatory celibacy policy. Previously headquartered in Iran, thousands of MEK members were relocated to Albania between 2013 and 2016 at the behest of the U.S., whose bidding Tirana is forever eager to do. The group now operates out of a heavily fortified camp in the Balkan nation, where members are punished for any sexual thoughts they might have and democracy otherwise flourishes (*Ibid.*).

137 See "A textile factory with a difference." *The Economist*, 21 May 2016. https://www.economist.com/middle-east-and-africa/2016/05/21/a-textile-factory-with-a-difference

138 Mazzetti, Mark. "U.S. Finds Iran Halted Its Nuclear Arms Effort in 2003." *New York Times*, 4 December 2007. https://www.nytimes.com/2007/12/04/world/middleeast/04intel.html

Satan and to assign me a guide for merely one out of 14 days. In Esfahan, I encountered the usual "we hate the American government but not the American people" rhetoric as well as some more unique reactions to my nationality, such as a bazaar merchant who burst into hysterical laughter for a period of several minutes.

My short-term friends in the city included a bookseller named Hadi who invited me to a weekly book fair in an underground parking lot, where I arrived at 9 a.m. to find droves of people streaming out of the entrance with garbage bags full of books, just like happens in America (not). Hadi intercepted me and conducted me to his table along the far wall, where his English-language offerings ranged from Mao Tse-tung and Ho Chi Minh to *KGB: The Secret Work of Soviet Secret Agents* to *Peg Bracken's Instant Etiquette Book* and the 1973 title *The Fragrance of Beauty*, penned by Joyce Landorf, whose author bio defined her as not only a "radiant beauty[,] homemaker and a career woman" but also a "singer who has recorded several albums—'Peace Through the Lord,' 'It's Great To Be Alive,' and her newest, 'Joyce.'" Among other credentials were "numerous Outstanding Service Awards from the U.S. Military for appearances around the world." I was forcibly given various texts as well as a giant hardback Farsi-English translation of the great Persian poet Sa'di, to augment the joys of dragging my suitcase.

Another companion was Hamid, a former volleyball player turned carpet shop employee, and a maker of illicit wine. Like many other young men I met in Esfahan, he was an aficionado of the couchsurfing phenomenon, whereby they and their couches or spare rooms hosted foreign visitors to the land. In addition to the array of traditional tapestries on display at his shop off of Esfahan's gleaming Naghsh-e Jahan Square were two carpets woven by Afghan refugees in Iran, which featured patterns incorporating warplanes, guns, and tanks—further evidence that, for all my bitching and moaning about not having a culture, there were loads of people with far greater complaints to register with the universe.

Though harboring zero love for the Iranian theocracy, Hamid also had many colorful expletives for the American regime, and furthermore contended that Western Iranophobes would be much safer in the Islamic Republic than in their own countries—unless, he added on second thought, they were run over by a car. Having experienced several near-martyrdoms myself as a pedestrian in Esfahan, I had to concur.

One sunny morning, Hamid took me running in a park along the (currently waterless) river, where assorted smartly dressed elderly gentlemen were experimenting cautiously on public exercise equipment. Following our jog, the gentlemen and I were put to shame when Hamid decided to execute a series of upper body feats on some bars. His volleyball career had lamentably been cut short, he explained, thanks to U.S. sanctions, which had caused funding for sports teams to plummet in addition to unleashing all manner of other, more life-threatening hardships.

Consider a 2013 *New York Times* intervention by Iranian American filmmaker and writer Beheshteh Farshneshani, who reviewed some of the repercussions of sanctions over the past year and a half alone: "[Iranian] families living in poverty rose from 22 to more than 40 percent . . . and the price of food regularly consumed by Iranians—for example, milk, tea, fruits and vegetables—skyrocketed. Moreover, the health of millions of Iranians has been compromised due to the shortage of western medical drugs and supplies."[139]

---

139 "In Iran, Sanctions Hurt the Wrong People." *New York Times*, 22 January 2014. https://www. nytimes.com/roomfordebate/2013/11/19/sanctions-successes-and-failures/in-iran-sanctions-hurt-the-wrong-people

While the U.S. prefers to paint sanctions as a supremely civilized form of diplomacy and the obvious responsibility of the global policeman, they in fact constitute war—as, again, was most vividly underscored in 1996 when Bill Clinton's Ambassador to the UN applauded the sanctions-based extermination of half a million Iraqi children: "We think the price is worth it."[140]

Nor, of course, did sanctions on Iran disappear on account of Barack Obama's nuclear deal, despite the torrent of right-wing apocalyptic squawking. Now, with Donald Trump at the helm and the likes of John "Bomb Iran" Bolton safely on board, there's little danger of any such Mullah-Appeasement Schemes recurring in the near future—not that Hillary Clinton hadn't been open to the idea of "totally obliterat[ing]" Iran.[141]

I departed Esfahan for Beirut on the morning of November 4, which, as it turned out, was the anniversary of the 1979 student takeover of the U.S. embassy in Tehran and the launch of the hostage crisis—a reaction to America's persistent chummy relations with the recently deposed shah, purchaser extraordinaire of American weapons. In his *History of Modern Iran*, scholar Ervand Abrahamian notes: "Arms dealers joked that the shah devoured their manuals in much the same way as other men read *Playboy*."[142] The Iranian Revolution put a tragic stop to this lucrative arrangement, and since 1979 Iran has been in American crosshairs for

---

140   For video clip see "Democracy Now! Confronts Madeleine Albright on the Iraq Sanctions: Was It Worth the Price?" *Democracy Now!*, 30 July 2004.

141   For Bolton, see "To Stop Iran's Bomb, Bomb Iran." *New York Times*, 26 March 2015. https://www.nytimes.com/2015/03/26/opinion/to-stop-irans-bomb-bomb-iran.html. For Clinton, see Morgan, David. "Clinton says U.S. could 'totally obliterate' Iran." *Reuters*, 22 April 2008. https://www.reuters.com/article/us-usa-politics-iran/clinton-says-u-s-could-totally-obliterate-iran-idUSN2224332720080422

142   Abrahamian, Ervand. *A History of Modern Iran*. Cambridge: Cambridge University Press, 2008, p. 124.

the unspeakable crime of noncompliance with U.S.-Israeli designs in the region. Any respect for Iran's control over its own destiny and resources went out the window in 1953, when the Americans and British perpetrated a coup against Prime Minister Mohammad Mossadegh, who had been under the impression that Iranian oil belonged to Iran.

According to Senator Ted Cruz, November 4 is officially celebrated in Iran as "Death to America Day"—a useful soundbite, no doubt, in terms of riling up xenophobic passions in the U.S. but apparently not properly publicized in Iran itself; the young man who drove me to the airport, at least, had not gotten the memo, as he continued to insist that "America good."[143] And while "Death to America" may indeed be a stock slogan of the Islamic Republic, it seems a fair enough retort to a country that consistently kills.

* * *

Granted, the U.S. was by this point pretty much dead to me, as I had determined from periodic visits that it was in the interest of my sanity to avoid the country altogether. Frida Kahlo once observed: "I find that Americans completely lack sensibility and good taste. They are boring, and they all have faces like unbaked rolls."[144] And yet this, perhaps, is the least of the problems.

For an introduction to the ills of the tasteless nation, one need go no further than airport passport control, a delightfully criminalizing experience

---

143 Cruz's notions on Iranian holidays are quoted in a press release on his official Senate website: "ICYMI: Sen. Cruz: Obama Administration Cannot Defend A Deal That Will Lead To Iran Acquiring Nuclear Weapons." 12 March 2015. https://www.cruz.senate.gov/?p=press_release&id=2258

144 Quoted in Tuchman, Phyllis. "Frida Kahlo." *Smithsonian Magazine*, November 2002. https://www.smithsonianmag.com/arts-culture/frida-kahlo-70745811/?all

that leaves one with the sneaking suspicion that America's customs and border agents are in fact not genetically human. Needless to say, the U.S. welcome can be a great deal more traumatic for noncitizens and/or persons suspected of Arab/Muslim identity. I myself can confirm more hospitable reception by immigration personnel everywhere from the Number One State Sponsor of Terrorism to the Number One Producer of Drug Dealers and Rapists.[145]

Before I definitively wrote off the homeland as an acceptable travel destination, obstacles to smooth U.S. entry had ranged from having visited Syria—for which activity the explanation "I have friends in Syria" was deemed insufficient ("Why do you have friends in Syria?")—to the matter of my inability to answer the question "Where do you live?" in any sort of remotely coherent, less-than-super-sketchy fashion. Obviously, in the end I was always admitted to the country with passport in tow, the pages of which were emblazoned with inspiring reminders ranging from "The God who gave us life, gave us liberty at the same time" (Thomas Jefferson) to "…That this nation, under God, shall have a new birth of freedom"

---

145 "Foremost state sponsor of terrorism" is one of America's pet designations for Iran (Lee, Matthew. "Iran still top state sponsor of terrorism, U.S. report says." Associated Press, 19 July 2017.   https://www.pbs.org/newshour/world/iran-still-top-state-sponsor-terrorism-u-s-report-says)—although it's not clear how Iran has achieved this distinction when it's not the one sponsoring the day-to-day terrorization of Palestinians, among numerous other human populations. The U.S. is the one doing that, just as the U.S. is the one inflicting terror-by-drone on communities from Pakistan to Somalia and backing the Saudi-Emirati slaughter-starvation in Yemen, a war that has seen such individual acts of terror as the bombing of 40 children on a school bus ("Elbagir, Nima and Salma Abdelaziz and Ryan Browne and Barbara Arvanitidis and Laura Smith-Spark. "Bomb that killed 40 children in Yemen was supplied by the U.S.." CNN, 17 August 2018. https://edition.cnn.com/2018/08/17/middleeast/us-saudi-yemen-bus-strike-intl/index.html). The drug dealer-rapist designation is Trump's assessment of the nation of Mexico, used to justify his border wall vision and other sociopathic initiatives ("'Drug dealers, criminals, rapists': What Trump thinks of Mexicans." BBC News, 31 August 2016. https://www.bbc.com/news/av/world-us-canada-37230916/drug-dealers-criminals-rapists-what-trump-thinks-of-mexicans).

(Abraham Lincoln, and to hell once again with separation of church and state) to "The cause of freedom is not the cause of a race or a sect, a party or a class—it is the cause of humankind, the very birthright of humanity" (Anna Julia Cooper, black feminist born in 1858).

The inclusion of this final (most accurate) sentiment certainly spices up the passport, but it's presumptuous coming from a government that—more than a century and a half after Cooper's birth—continues to deny humanity to numerous categories of humankind. This same government also happens to enforce a domestic system characterized by structural racism and a criminalization of poverty, meaning that much of the United States' own population has yet to be granted its "birthright."[146] As for other manifestations of "freedom" and "liberty" in God's favorite nation, these might comprise the freedom to carry a firearm, the freedom to be shot by someone carrying a firearm, and the freedom to enter into eternal debt in exchange for education, housing, nontoxic food items, and health care.[147] As George W. Bush once eloquently put it: "Freedom is winning."[148]

---

146 See, for example, "Criminalization of Poverty as a Driver of Poverty in the United States." Human Rights Watch, 4 October 2017. https://www.hrw.org/news/2017/10/04/criminaliza-tion-poverty-driver-poverty-united-states: "After a police officer in Ferguson, Missouri shot and killed [unarmed black teenager] Michael Brown, the Department of Justice released a report exposing how the city routinely and disproportionately targeted poor, black residents with high fees and fines on low-level offenses, and then enforced those debts through judicial authority, warrants, and incarceration. As of December 2014, over 16,000 people had outstanding arrest warrants in a city with a total population of approximately 21,000."

147 In some cases, like that of Kennesaw, Georgia, possession of a firearm is not a freedom but rather a requirement: Jiménez, Omar. "In this American town, guns are required by law." *CNN*, 7 March 2018. https://edition.cnn.com/2018/03/06/us/kennesaw-georgia-gun-ownership/index .html

148 "Full text: President Bush's speech on U.S. security." *The Guardian*, 7 June 2002. https://www .theguardian.com/world/2002/jun/07/usa.september11

In December 2017, the United Nations special rapporteur on extreme poverty and human rights found that, despite the constant theme of "American exceptionalism," the contemporary U.S. has "proved itself to be exceptional in far more problematic ways that are shockingly at odds with its immense wealth" and in fact conducive to "public squalor," with no less than "one quarter of youth living in poverty." Among the myriad issues highlighted was the "role of corporations in preventing rational policy-making and advocating against reforms in order to maintain their profits at the expense of the poorest members of society." Case in point: "the corporations running private for-profit prisons."

While the U.S. "spends more on national defense than China, Saudi Arabia, Russia, [the] United Kingdom, India, France, and Japan combined," the report notes, U.S. infant mortality rates were as of 2013 "the highest in the developed world." Furthermore: "Americans can expect to live shorter and sicker lives, compared to people living in any other rich democracy, and the 'health gap' between the U.S. and its peer countries continues to grow."[149] To be sure, none of this information is enormously bewildering given U.S. leaders' prioritization of corporate freedom and the health of the arms industry over the actual health of the people allegedly being protected via gargantuan defense budgets ($717 billion for Fiscal Year 2019).[150]

---

149 "Statement on Visit to the USA, by Professor Philip Alston, United Nations Special Rapporteur on extreme poverty and human rights." United Nations Office of the High Commissioner for Human Rights, 15 December 2017. https://www.ohchr.org/EN/NewsEvents/Pages/DisplayNews.aspx?NewsID=22533&LangID=E

150 "$717 Billion Budget Critical to Rebuilding, Restoring Readiness, Pentagon Officials Say." U.S. Department of Defense, 1 August 2018. https://dod.defense.gov/News/Article/Article/1591131/717-billion-budget-critical-to-rebuilding-restoring-readiness-pentagon-official/

Another perk, then, of evading the homeland at all cost is that the risk of pauperizing oneself for life in the event of medical emergency is much less in other locales. In Venezuela in 2009, Amelia and I availed ourselves of free health care services on various occasions, primarily for the novelty of being attended to in a context of compassionate solidarity rather than one of economic exploitation—an arrangement I dare say inspired greater feelings of personal security than did, say, the knowledge that my government could nuke the world at any second.

In 2006 in Cuba—another territory where health care was viewed as a right instead of a grand moneymaking opportunity—we also had free checkups, although the Cuban heart surgeon at whose Havana home we were staying recommended his preferred *santería* priestess to us for additional feedback. The priestess diagnosed me with some internal pelvic problem requiring treatment in the form of a ritual with eggs and *aguardiente*. I assumed the procedure would be pelvically invasive, but it turned out that I simply had to sit next to a glass of *aguardiente* while the priestess rubbed a hardboiled egg on my stomach and swatted me with some herbs. I was charged a dollar to cover the cost of the materials. As I had not been aware of any problem in the first place, I was in no position to judge the effectiveness of the intervention, but there were certainly more boring ways to spend a couple of hours.

Other internal issues were resolved in Turkey, where in 2007 I obtained a most affordable abortion performed by a doctor in Fethiye named Nezih, who alternately sang songs and told me about all of his village-woman patients who unlike me were tough and needed no anesthetic whatsoever. In Tajikistan in 2016, I checked myself into a Soviet-era sanatorium in the mountains for a couple of nights for a nominal fee, where the only English-speaking person was a maniacal Christian Zionist and former U.S.

resident who kept trying to lure me to church with her in the Tajik capital of Dushanbe. Fleeing her presence, I embraced the communication barrier and went wherever the sanatorium attendants pushed me—which is how I ended up in a room with a mass of elderly nude Tajik women and a toilet-seat-type contraption designed to spray water into one's vagina. Retroactive research revealed that the uniqueness of the water in question had to do with its radioactive radon content.

In an extract from *Holidays in Soviet Sanatoriums* published at *The Calvert Journal*, Maryam Omidi writes that, "[u]nlike western vacations, which Soviets perceived as vulgar pursuits characterized by conspicuous consumption and idleness," holidays in the USSR were meant "to provide rest and recuperation, so citizens could return to work with renewed diligence and productivity." Under Joseph Stalin, Omidi notes, "the 'right to rest' was enshrined in the 1936 constitution," and sanatoriums were "designed in opposition to the decadence of European spa towns . . . as well as to the west's bourgeois consumer practices. Every detail of sanatorium life, from architecture to entertainment, was intended to edify workers while encouraging communion with other guests and with nature."[151]

The debatable effectiveness of radioactive spray to one's nether regions notwithstanding, such remedies are undoubtedly cooler than the go-to capitalist approach of medicating everyone senseless. Moreover, a bit of worker edification and socio-environmental communion would prove therapeutic for a bumbling, unbaked-roll-faced population deficient in the

---

151 "Holidays in Soviet Sanatoriums: The weird and wonderful wellness palaces of the USSR." *The Calvert Journal*, 19 October 2017. http://www.calvertjournal.com/features/show/9100/holidays-in-soviet-sanatoriums-ussr-tourism-photography

natural grace that often attends symbiotic relationships with the earth and other living things.

* * *

My exile from the U.S. has been facilitated by the fact that—following the deaths of my non-psychotic set of grandparents and my parents' own subsequent defection from the country—I no longer have significant roots there. As a child, I was close to my father's younger sister, who suffered from an unhealthy obsession with the Democratic Party and whose idea of revolution was—literally—allowing Soviet victims of communism access to American blue jeans. This aunt disapproved of my wandering, and decided that her position was vindicated when I received a minor punch to the head after feeling compelled to intervene in a bar fight in Spain in 2003.

When I paid what was to be the final visit to her mansion outside Washington, D.C. in 2004, she informed me that my dead grandmother would have been ashamed of me and advised me to open a bakery with all due haste—this being the standard key to success for someone who did not bake. I dragged my suitcase dramatically down the side of the road for two hours to the Bethesda metro stop, and that was the end of that.

My brother in the Special Forces continued to reside in the States, of course, and during our rare interactions supplied anecdotes from military life, such as a training session in which he and his fellow trainees played a game of good guys and bad guys. The latter were denoted by a garment resembling a keffiyeh, and—lest there remain any doubt about the nature of the enemy—the instructors provided the good guys with encouragement along the lines of "get the fucking Arabs." From my brother's later tours in Afghanistan, Iraq, and Syria, I learned that it was sometimes possible to purposefully misfire projectiles in order to inflict human and infrastructural damage you weren't necessarily authorized to inflict by your superiors, and that most terrorists were named Mohammad and Abdul. No doubt relatives of Afghan wedding attendees slaughtered by U.S. bombs begged to differ on that account.[152]

On the same trip to D.C. during which I failed to open a bakery, I dropped by Arlington National Cemetery to pay my respects with a couple of beers at the gravesite of my grandfather, decorated war veteran and fan of Heineken. Although the public alcohol consumption and ensuing placement of beer bottles around the tombstone miraculously went unnoticed, I was castigated by a policeman for crossing slightly to the left of the crosswalk on a road with zero vehicles on it. And while institutionalized anal retentiveness among U.S. cops obviously doesn't compare to other kinds of behavioral repertoires for which the guardians of law and order are known—like shooting pregnant Native American women and mentally ill persons—the crosswalk castigation might just symbolize the oppressively monotonous spirit of America, where the sanctity of THE RULES and the absolute imperative of staying within the lines serves to distract from the possibility that our brief and insignificant time on this planet might be rendered considerably more pleasant for all involved were alienation from the human condition not the modus operandi.[153]

---

152 See Engelhardt, Tom. "The U.S. Has Bombed at Least Eight Wedding Parties Since 2001." *The Nation*, 20 December 2013. https://www.thenation.com/article/us-has-bombed-least-eight-wedding-parties-2001/. Of course, Afghan wedding participants are not the only ones eligible for being bombed to smithereens by the U.S.; see also Draper, Lucy. "The Wedding That Became a Funeral: U.S. Still Silent One Year on From Deadly Yemen Drone Strike." *Newsweek*, 12 December 2014. https://www.newsweek.com/wedding-became-funeral-us-still-silent-one-year-deadly-yemen-drone-strike-291403

153 For police shootings, see Woodard, Stephanie. "The Police Killings No One Is Talking About." *In These Times*, 17 October 2016. http://inthesetimes.com/features/native_american_police_killings_native_lives_matter.html

I've got plenty of other flashbacks, too, that encapsulate the essence of America for me, many of them having to do with 9/11, the eternal defining tragedy of the homeland and the excuse for America's perpetual wars. There was that time, for example, that acquaintances of mine in Austin, Texas, ordered mass quantities of KFC—"comfort food," they called it—to cope with the attacks on the World Trade Center 3,000-ish kilometers away, or the time that the Marriott offered its clientele the following emotional experience: "In remembrance of those we lost on 9/11 the hotel will provide complimentary coffee and mini muffins from 8:45 – 9:15 a.m."[154] And yet, beneath all the fried chicken and muffins, there was always something far more sinister at play: the political exploitation of mass bloodshed and the notion of national victimhood to justify mass aggression abroad and the shedding of far greater quantities of innocent blood.

Meanwhile, though it is relatively easy to take the American out of America, it is generally more challenging to exorcise the huffy, customer-is-always-right sense of entitlement from the American. Supplementary evidence of this can most lamentably be found in my own track record, which has included episodes such as a brief shit fit at the train ticket office in Sri Lanka when the concept of the orderly line—suddenly all-important!—was being ignored. This fit was conducted with full awareness that it was not the most endearing comportment in a country that had in recent history played host to the massacre of tens of thousands of Tamil civilians whose earthly rights were irreconcilable with the vision of homeland sponsored by the Sri Lankan

---

154 See Stableford, Dylan. "AT&T, Marriott, others apologize for tacky and outrageous 9/11 tie-ins." *Yahoo News*, 11 September 2013. https://www.yahoo.com/news/9-11-fails-never-forget-185206681.html

powers that be.[155] Hundreds of thousands were additionally uprooted by the country's civil war, the moral of the story being that there were far more severe dilemmas to choose from in the present environment than whether I was second or seventh in the queue.[156]

International meandering has brought me into contact with my fair share of fans of the U.S., as well as people who are simply of the opinion that because the U.S. is my country I should like it. I've also had the opportunity to explore George W. Bush Street in the Albanian capital of Tirana, though I did not make it to the George W. Bush statue in the Albanian village of Fushë-Krujë, the Hillary Clinton statue in Sarandë, or the city of Kamëz, where Donald Trump not only has a boulevard named for him but has also been made an honorary citizen. The American dream is, however, hardly beguiling across the board. In Sarajevo in 2018, I spoke with a middle-aged woman named Lejla, a vendor of bee products who had fled to Missouri during the Bosnian war of the 1990s. She returned two decades later, she told me, for reasons that included being creeped out by the ubiquitous security presence in the U.S.—no small statement from a native of a place synonymous with snipers as well as the site of the longest siege of a capital city in modern history.[157]

---

155 According to one UN estimate, some 40,000 Tamils were killed in the Sri Lankan army's final offensive alone ("UN Human Rights Council urges Sri Lanka war crimes court." *BBC News*, 16 September 2015. https://www.bbc.com/news/world-asia-34266471). Some estimates are lower; others are higher.

156 For the displacement of hundreds of thousands, see Mitchell, Charlotte. "Q&A: Sri Lanka's civil war through a Tamil lens." *Al Jazeera*, 31 January 2018. https://www.aljazeera.com/indepth/features/qa-sri-lanka-civil-war-tamil-lens-180131121436527.html

157 See Fisk, Robert. "The fisherman in Sarajevo told tales of past wars—and warned me of ones to come." *The Independent*, 13 July 2018. https://www.independent.co.uk/voices/sarajevo-bosnian-war-muslim-croat-serb-fisherman-robert-fisk-a8443941.html

Then there was the Peace Community of San José de Apartadó in remote northwestern Colombia, one of my hitchhiking destinations with Amelia in 2009, where residents were under no illusions that America might be a place where dreams were made.[158] Founded in 1997 on the rejection of cooperation with any and all armed actors on the domestic scene—namely the Colombian military, paramilitaries, and leftist Revolutionary Armed Forces of Colombia (FARC)—the Peace Community had thus far suffered 184 assassinations out of a population of approximately 1,500. In other words, no one was willing to leave the Peace Community in peace. The vast majority of crimes were attributed to the military-paramilitary partnership, with the army's 17th Brigade accused of rapes, forced displacements, and other abuses.

The United States' contributions to the mix included giant influxes of military aid to Colombia under the pretense of fighting a war on drugs and terror, while the great American banana company Chiquita Brands International had previously lent a helping hand by paying a bunch

---

158 Amelia and I learned of the Peace Community from a passage in Forrest Hylton's *Evil Hour in Colombia* (New York: Verso, 2006) and made it one of our must-see destinations on an otherwise pliant hitchhiking itinerary. Along with Syria—where motorists were unsure as to what we were doing on the side of the road with our thumbs but would sometimes stop and ask—Colombia was one of our slightly more challenging hitchhiking experiences given people's frequent reluctance to pick us up. Some Colombians suggested that this was perhaps a result of recent robbery schemes involving female hitchhikers. During one particularly hopeless stretch by the roadside, we resorted to designing colorful placards featuring the name of the next town amidst rainbows and flowers. We then resorted to drawing stop signs in red marker and placing ourselves in the middle of the road, but vehicles simply swerved around us. We even tried appealing to police at anti-narcotics checkpoints in the hopes that they might wield their authority on our behalf, but many folks appeared to trust the police even less than they trusted us. Of course, we were always picked up in the end, and managed to traverse Colombia twice.

of money to a Colombian paramilitary outfit categorized as a terrorist organization by the U.S..[159]

Although Amelia and I had not managed to notify the Peace Community in advance of our arrival, we were graciously and unsuspiciously welcomed and provided with accommodation and food for a week, and the community members took turns shepherding us around to the various activities that were underway, including the cultivation of miniature bananas and cacao by collective work groups. One of the founders of the community, a woman with two grey braids named María Brígida González, filled us in on relevant history such as the 2005 killing of her 15-year-old daughter Eliseña and five other persons by members of the 17th Brigade. The victims, murdered in their sleep, were painted as FARC combatants by the army.

González contended that one objective of armed attacks on unarmed *campesinos* was to "sow terror" in order to uproot human obstacles to the exploitation of the territory's numerous resources. Now, nearly a decade later, the Peace Community is still under regular assault—despite the supposed onset of official "peace" in Colombia—and *campesino* efforts to put down roots in a tranquil bit of homeland continue to be at odds with the belligerent right-wing orientation of the state.

Not long after our visit to San José de Apartadó, Thomas Friedman produced the revelation that Colombia was "one of the great democratic success

---

159 "Chiquita admits to paying Colombia terrorists." *Associated Press*, 15 March 2007. http://www.nbcnews.com/id/17615143/ns/business-us_business/t/chiquita-admits-paying-colombia-terrorists/#.W_Boq3pKh-V. Chiquita Brands is a descendant of the United Fruit Company, whose very important interests provoked the notorious 1954 coup against Guatemala's Jacobo Árbenz—lest there be any doubt that U.S. corporations go bananas for the right wing.

stories," a position the country had somehow achieved even while playing host to more trade unionist murders than the rest of the world combined.[160] The *Wall Street Journal* editorial board's Mary Anastasia O'Grady—a Colombian paramilitary in her own right and propagator of the claim that the Peace Community is a front for the FARC—meanwhile popped down to Bogotá to swoon over "The Man Who Saved Colombia," i.e. outgoing president Álvaro Uribe, who told her that Colombia was not in a civil war at all "but rather in a struggle against 'terrorists sponsored by narco-trafficking.'"[161] This is the same Uribe, of course, who appeared on a 1991 U.S. Defense Intelligence Agency list of "the more important Colombian narco-traffickers contracted by the Colombian narcotic cartels."[162]

*   *   *

---

160 For Friedman, see "As Ugly as It Gets." *New York Times*, 25 May 2010. https://www.nytimes.com/2010/05/26/opinion/26friedman.html. For reality, see Maher, David. *Civil War and Uncivil Development: Economic Globalization and Political Violence in Colombia and Beyond.* London: Palgrave Macmillan, 2018, p. 102: "During the first five years of the Uribe administration, 2,402 violations against trade unions were recorded, including threats, homicide, arbitrary detention, harassment and forced displacement, with more unionists assassinated in Colombia than anywhere else in the world combined."

161 See O'Grady, Mary Anastasia. "The FARC and the 'Peace Community.'" *Wall Street Journal*, 13 December 2009. https://www.wsj.com/articles/SB10001424052748704517504574590200781231082, and O'Grady, Mary Anastasia. "The Man Who Saved Colombia." *Wall Street Journal*, 29 May 2010. https://www.wsj.com/articles/SB10001424052748704717004575268763528382500

162 See "U.S. intelligence listed Colombian President Uribe among 'Important Colombian narco-traffickers' in 1991." The National Security Archive, 1 August 2004. https://nsarchive2.gwu.edu/NSAEBB/NSAEBB131/. Contrary to O'Grady's fantasies, there are a whole hell of a lot of Colombians who would not consider themselves "saved" by Uribe—such as the 10,000 or so civilians now estimated to have been slaughtered during the "false positives" affair by the Colombian military, which was under pressure from the Uribe administration to show some progress in the country's own "war on terror" and thereby justify continued gargantuan U.S. military aid (Eskauriatza, Seb. "Colombia's 'cash-for-kills' victims could number 10,000 civilians." *The Independent*, 17 June 2018. https://www.independent.co.uk/news/world/politics/colombia-cash-for-kills-murders-military-guerilla-forces-conflict-civilian-a8364906.html). The

In *Drinking Mare's Milk on the Roof of the World: Wandering the Globe from Azerbaijan to Zanzibar*, Tom Lutz—editor-in-chief of the *Los Angeles Review of Books*—reflects on his own wanderlust: "Am I running toward something? Running away?" He continues: "Whatever the motivation, the essence of travel is to be somewhere else, to be somewhere distinctly not home . . . As Pico Iyer says, we travel until we come home, and then, if we are lucky, at home, in stillness, we write."

This, to be sure, is one of the less grating excerpts of a book that recounts such adventures as the time Francine, the black maid at Lutz's B&B in Pretoria, South Africa, "allowed herself the slightest smile" because Lutz was "eating poor people's food." The charming scene came about after Lutz had driven his rental car to the poor-people's-food place for takeout, being propositioned by prostitutes along the way and "thinking AIDS, AIDS, AIDS, AIDS, AIDS."[163]

---

corpses were passed off as guerrillas, while the killers were showered with bonus pay, holiday time, and other perks. O'Grady based her Peace Community article, published the same year as our visit, on an interview with a former FARC commander—alias "Samir"—who had deserted the organization and begun collaborating with the government (a change of course that was presumably handsomely rewarded). The summary of the article informs us that, in so-called "peace communities" in Colombia, "peace-niks helped the terrorists"—as if the Colombian military-paramilitary alliance needed any more encouragement to attack. In the article itself, O'Grady tells us that, "[a]ccording to Samir, the peace community helped the FARC in its effort to tag the Colombian military as a violator of human rights." While the military shouldn't really have required any help in that regard, O'Grady's quite literally lethal journalism serves as an illustrative example of the aggressiveness with which the U.S. media has been known to leap onto the bandwagon of war, reducing to nothing the lives of people in Colombia and beyond with a mere stroke of the pen.

163 Lutz, Tom. *Drinking Mare's Milk on the Roof of the World: Wandering the Globe from Azerbaijan to Zanzibar.* New York: OR Books, 2016.

What I myself might be running toward I haven't the faintest clue, although on the bright side I have at least learned more about the state of the world than I ever did from that obscene swindle known as college education in the U.S. And while the constant expectation is that I will eventually settle down somewhere or at least erect a home base—as though the point is indeed to "travel until we come home"—there can be something oddly settling about motion itself. Bruce Chatwin's *In Patagonia*, for example, quotes ethnographer Father Martin Gusinde on the indigenous Yaghans of Tierra del Fuego: "They resemble fidgety birds of passage, who feel happy and inwardly calm only when they are on the move."[164]

Not that inner peace is always, or ever, the name of my game. One byproduct of my itinerant lifestyle is, unsurprisingly, a scattered sense of self—particularly when the self has opted to scatter its belongings across various countries without keeping proper track of what ends up where. The temptation to conduct parallel lives in different landscapes can furthermore land the self in a fair heap of trouble, specifically in the romantic arena. The centrality of *yerba mate* to my own existence adds another layer of logistical considerations to my travel planning, as I must always allow for periodic stops in countries where it is possible to stockpile this life-giving elixir.

I can't be sure about the Yaghans, but I'd wager that their motion-based contentedness may have been derived in part from the act of communal movement, whereas my own traditional solitude on the road has bred intriguing neurotic tendencies such as the regular instigation of verbal

---

164   Chatwin, Bruce. *In Patagonia*. New York: Penguin, 1977, p. 137.

fights with myself in public. The panic attacks that defined my days in the U.S., on the other hand, are gone.

Nor, of course, did the Yaghans get their birds-of-passage fix by flying around for 80-something hours polluting the planet on a Mexico-Canada-Hong Kong-India-Sri Lanka travel trajectory specially crafted to bypass the U.S. and its more convenient airports. Indeed, while I may view a life of voluntary permanent transit as personally sustainable, the unsustainable nature of popular modes of transport in the context of the current planetary meltdown would seem to indicate otherwise. Involuntary transit is, however, another story; as *The Independent* noted in October 2017, a new study suggested that "[m]ore than a billion people could be forced to flee their homes because of global warming."[165]

More than a tad of the blame for the annihilation of the environment naturally goes to the vanguard of the capitalist system—the United States of America—which, under the present leadership of the man who denounced climate change as a Chinese hoax, is attaining ever more transparent levels of madness. So while some eco-friendlier peregrinatory adjustments are no doubt in order on my part, so is the overthrow of the entire putrid system itself.

In the meantime, should I ever decide to reverse my self-imposed exile, I have a standing invitation to appear on the television show of *Fox News* superstar Tucker Carlson, who originally asked me on in 2016 to discuss the death of Fidel Castro. I responded, as one does, that I was at a slumber

---

165 Griffin, Andrew. "Climate change could force more than a billion people to flee their homes, says major health report." *The Independent*, 31 October 2017. https://www.independent .co.uk/news/science/climate-change-global-warming-refugees-migrants-displacement-lan-cet-study-a8028341.html

party in Yugoslavia and had to milk the cow, leading to an email back-and-forth between Carlson and me over various days:

> *HIM: As it happens, we've got a spare camera crew and a satellite truck at our Belgrade bureau and would be happy to meet you at any cow barn in the country for an interview. Just send your coordinates and milking schedule and we'll be there.*

> *ME: Ok awesome I'm in Bosnia though and there are Muslims, but anyway here are driving directions from Belgrade:*
> 1. *Head in a southwesterly direction for roughly 504 kilometers (313.17 miles)*
> 2. *Don't stop when you reach the Adriatic shoreline.*

> *HIM: Alright now I really want to interview you, about anything. How about Tom Friedman? I'll bet I agreed with at least 80 percent of your book. Let me know when you're in Washington.*

Ah, the ties that bind.

Meanwhile, other more dated correspondence on issues of homeland and roaming exists courtesy of the Right Honourable Lady Mary Wortley Montagu—English aristocrat, seasoned traveler, and dedicated letter-writer—who in a missive dated October 1718 offered the following assessment:

> ...I cannot help looking with partial eyes on my native land. That partiality was certainly given us by nature to prevent rambling, the effect of an ambitious thirst after knowledge which we are not formed to enjoy. All we get by it is fruitless desire of mixing the different pleasures and conveniences which are given to different parts of the world and cannot meet in any one of them . . . I think the honest English squire more happy who verily believes the Greek wines less delicious than

March beer, that the African fruits have not so fine a flavour as golden pippins, and the becàfiguas of Italy are not so well tasted as a rump of beef, and that, in short, there is no perfect enjoyment of this life out of Old England. I pray God I may think so for the rest of my life, and since I must be contented with our scanty allowance of daylight, that I may forget the enlivening sun of Constantinople.[166]

And though I certainly get what she's saying, some of us require a bit more sunlight.

---

166 Wortley Montagu, Lady Mary. *The Turkish Embassy Letters*. London: Virago Press, 1994, pp. 164–5.